Presented to

Kelly

by

Isa

date

7/2/02

Happy 17th
Birthday!

God's
      Promises®

roCk

(youR WorLd)

J. COUNTRYMAN

NASHVILLE, TENNESSEE

Scriptures quoted from *The Holy Bible,* New Century Version,
copyright © 1987, 1988, 1991 by Word Publishing, Nashville,
Tennessee 37214. Used by permission.

God's Promises® is a registered trademark of J. Countryman®,
a division of Thomas Nelson, Inc.

J. Countryman® is a trademark of Thomas Nelson Inc.

Project editor: Jenny Baumgartner

Cover design by Kirk DouPonce, Uttley/DouPonce
DesignWorks, Sisters, Oregon

ISBN: 0-8499-9507-8

Printed and bound in the United States of America

www.jcountryman.com

Contents

Jesus
Is Your . . .

Jesus Is Your Savior

He saved us because of his mercy. It was not because of good deeds we did to be right with him. He saved us through the washing that made us new people through the Holy Spirit. God poured out richly upon us that Holy Spirit through Jesus Christ our Savior.

Titus 3:5-6

We have seen and can testify that the Father sent his Son to be the Savior of the world.

1 John 4:14

My soul praises the Lord; my heart rejoices in God my Savior.

Luke 1:46b-47

The Son of Man came to find lost people and save them.

Luke 19:10

God loved the world so much that he gave his one and only Son so that whoever believes in him may not be lost, but have eternal life.

John 3:16

God makes people right with himself through their faith in Jesus Christ. This is true for all who believe in Christ, because all people are the same: All have sinned and are not good enough for God's glory, and all need to be made right with God by his grace, which is a free gift. They need to be made free from sin through Jesus Christ.

Romans 3:22-24

But God's mercy is great, and he loved us very much. Though we were spiritually dead because of the things we did against God, he gave us new life with Christ. You have been saved by God's grace.

Ephesians 2:4-5

I tell you the truth, whoever believes has eternal life.

John 6:47

If anyone belongs to Christ, there is a new creation. The old things have gone; everything is made new!

2 Corinthians 5:17

Jesus Is Your Lord

So God raised him to the highest place. God made his name greater than every other name so that every knee will bow to the name of Jesus—everyone in heaven, on earth, and under the earth. And everyone will confess that Jesus Christ is Lord and bring glory to God the Father.

Philippians 2:9-11

If you use your mouth to say, "Jesus is Lord," and if you believe in your heart that God raised Jesus from the dead, you will be saved. We believe with our hearts, and so we are made right with God. And we use our mouths to say that we believe, and so we are saved.

Romans 10:9-10

Why do you call me, "Lord, Lord," but do not do what I say?

Luke 6:46

Surely you know that when you give yourselves like slaves to obey someone, then you are really slaves of that person. The person you obey is your master. You can follow sin, which brings spiritual death, or you can obey God, which makes you right with him.

Romans 6:16

So brothers and sisters, since God has shown us great mercy, I beg you to offer your lives as a living sacrifice to him. Your offering must be only for God and pleasing to him, which is the spiritual way for you to worship. Do not change yourselves to be like the people of this world, but be changed within by a new way of thinking. Then you will be able to decide what God wants for you; you will know what is good and pleasing to him and what is perfect.

Romans 12:1-2

So, all the people of Israel should know this truly: God has made Jesus—the man you nailed to the cross—both Lord and Christ.

Acts 2:36

If we live, we are living for the Lord, and if we die, we are dying for the Lord. So living or dying, we belong to the Lord.

Romans 14:8

Praise the Lord, God our Savior, who helps us every day.

Psalm 68:19

But I am close to God, and that is good. The Lord God is my protection. I will tell all that you have done.

Psalm 73:28

Lord, you are kind and forgiving and have great love for those who call to you.

Psalm 86:5

The Lord God helps me, so I will not be ashamed. I will be determined, and I know I will not be disgraced.

Isaiah 50:7

Love the Lord your God with all your heart, all your soul, all your mind, and all your strength.

Mark 12:30

For David said this about him: "I keep the Lord before me always. Because he is close by my side, I will not be hurt."

Acts 2:25

Jesus Is Your Love

But God shows his great love for us in this way: Christ died for us while we were still sinners.

Romans 5:8

God loved the world so much that he gave his one and only Son so that whoever believes in him may not be lost, but have eternal life.

John 3:16

Dear friends, we should love each other, because love comes from God. Everyone who loves has become God's child and knows God. Whoever does not love does not know God, because God is love. This is how God showed his love to us: He sent his one and only Son into the world so that we could have life through him. This is what real love is: It is not our love for God; it is God's love for us in sending his Son to be the way to take away our sins. Dear friends, if God loved us that much we also should love each other. No one has ever seen God, but if we love each other, God lives in us, and his love is made perfect in us.

1 John 4:7-12

And so we know the love that God has for us, and we trust that love. God is love. Those who live in love live in God, and God lives in them. We love because God first loved us.

1 John 4:16, 19

I loved you as the Father loved me. Now remain in my love. I have obeyed my Father's commands, and I remain in his love. In the same way, if you obey my commands, you will remain in my love. I have told you these things so that you can have the same joy I have and so that your joy will be the fullest possible joy. This is my command: Love each other as I have loved you. The greatest love a person can show is to die for his friends. This is my command: Love each other.

John 15:9–13, 17

I pray that Christ will live in your hearts by faith and that your life will be strong in love and be built on love. And I pray that you and all God's holy people will have the power to understand the greatness of Christ's love—how wide and how long and how high and how deep that love is. Christ's love is greater than anyone can ever know, but I pray that you will be able to know that love. Then you can be filled with the fullness of God.

Ephesians 3:17–19

I love those who love me, and
those who seek me find me.

Proverbs 8:17

And from far away the Lord appeared to his people and said, "I love you people with a love that will last forever. That is why I have continued showing you kindness."

Jeremiah 31:3

And I will make you my promised bride forever. I will be good and fair; I will show you my love and mercy.

Hosea 2:19

Those who know my commands and obey them are the ones who love me, and my Father will love those who love me. I will love them and will show myself to them.

John 14:21

The Lord shows his true love every day. At night I have a song, and I pray to my living God.

Psalm 42:8

So these three things continue forever: faith, hope, and love. And the greatest of these is love.

1 Corinthians 13:13

Yes, I am sure that neither death, nor life, nor angels, nor ruling spirits, nothing now, nothing in the future, no powers, nothing above us, nothing below us, nor anything else in the whole world will ever be able to separate us from the love of God that is in Christ Jesus our Lord.

Romans 8:38-39

Jesus Is Your Peace

You, Lord, give true peace to those who depend on you, because they trust you.

Isaiah 26:3

Christ himself is our peace. He made both Jewish people and those who are not Jews one people. They were separated as if there were a wall between them, but Christ broke down that wall of hate by giving his own body.

Ephesians 2:14

A child has been born to us; God has given a son to us. He will be responsible for leading the people. His name will be Wonderful Counselor, Powerful God, Father Who Lives Forever, Prince of Peace. Power and peace will be in his kingdom and will continue to grow forever.

Isaiah 9:6–7a

The God who brings peace will soon defeat Satan and give you power over him. The grace of our Lord Jesus be with you.

Romans 16:20

Lord, all our success is because of what you have done, so give us peace.

Isaiah 26:12

Do what you learned and received from me, what I told you, and what you saw me do. And the God who gives peace will be with you.

Philippians 4:9

Since we have been made right with God by our faith, we have peace with God. This happened through our Lord Jesus Christ.

Romans 5:1

I go to bed and sleep in peace, because, Lord, only you keep me safe.

Psalm 4:8

> The **Lord** gives strength
> to his people; the Lord blesses
> his people with **peace**.
>
> Psalm 29:11

I leave you peace; my peace I give you. I do not give it to you as the world does. So don't let your hearts be troubled or afraid.

John 14:27

Jesus Is Your Deliverer

Then you will know the truth, and the truth will make you free. So if the Son makes you free, you will be truly free.

John 8:32, 36

The Lord God has put his Spirit in me, because the Lord has appointed me to tell the good news to the poor. He has sent me to comfort those whose hearts are broken, to tell the captives they are free, and to tell the prisoners they are released.

Isaiah 61:1

Through Christ Jesus the law of the Spirit that brings life made me free from the law that brings sin and death.

Romans 8:2

The Lord is the Spirit, and where the Spirit of the Lord is, there is freedom.

2 Corinthians 3:17

But now you are free from sin and have become slaves of God. This brings you a life that is only for God, and this gives you life forever.

Romans 6:22

The Lord has put his Spirit in me, because he appointed me to tell the Good News to the poor. He has sent me to tell the captives they are free and to tell the blind that they can see again. God sent me to free those who have been treated unfairly and to announce the time when the Lord will show his kindness.

Luke 4:18–19

Listen, I have given you power to walk on snakes and scorpions, power that is greater than the enemy has. So nothing will hurt you.

Luke 10:19

And those who believe will be able to do these things as proof: They will use my name to force out demons. They will speak in new languages.

Mark 16:17

My dear friends, many false prophets have gone out into the world. So do not believe every spirit, but test the spirits to see if they are from God. This is how you can know God's Spirit: Every spirit who confesses that Jesus Christ came to earth as a human is from God. And every spirit who refuses to say this about Jesus is not from God.

1 John 4:1–3a

Jesus Is Your Example

This is what you were called to do, because Christ suffered for you and gave you an example to follow. So you should do as he did.

1 Peter 2.21

Whoever says that he lives in God must live as Jesus lived.

1 John 2:6

You are God's children whom he loves, so try to be like him. Live a life of love just as Christ loved us and gave himself for us as a sweet-smelling offering and sacrifice to God.

Ephesians 5:1-2

In your lives you must think and act like Christ Jesus. Christ himself was like God in everything. But he did not think that being equal with God was something to be used for his own benefit. But he gave up his place with God and made himself nothing. He was born to be a man and became like a servant. And when he was living as a man, he humbled himself and was fully obedient to God, even when that caused his death—death on a cross.

Philippians 2:54

Whoever wants to become great among you must serve the rest of you like a servant. Whoever wants to become the first among you must serve all of you like a slave. In the same way, the Son of Man did not come to be served. He came to serve others and to give his life as a ransom for many people.

Mark 10:43-45

If I, your Lord and Teacher, have washed your feet, you also should wash each other's feet. I did this as an example so that you should do as I have done for you.

John 13:14-15

I give you a new command:
Love each other. You must love
each other as I have loved you.

John 13:34

This is how we know what real love is: Jesus gave his life for us. So we should give our lives for our brothers and sisters.

1 John 3:16

Christ accepted you, so you should accept each other, which will bring glory to God.

Romans 15:7

Get along with each other, and forgive each other. If someone does wrong to you, forgive that person because the Lord forgave you.

Colossians 3:13

Think about Jesus' example. He held on while wicked people were doing evil things to him. So do not get tired and stop trying.

Hebrews 12:3

Jesus Is Your Friend

I no longer call you servants, because a servant does not know what his master is doing. But I call you friends, because I have made known to you everything I heard from my Father. You did not choose me; I chose you.

John 15:15–16a

Some friends may ruin you,
but a real friend will be more
loyal than a brother.

Proverbs 18:24

"The mountains may disappear, and the hills may come to an end, but my love will never disappear; my promise of peace will not come to an end," says the Lord who shows mercy to you.

Isaiah 54:10

Come near to God, and God will come near to you. You sinners, clean sin out of your lives. You who are trying to follow God and the world at the same time, make your thinking pure.

James 4:8

If my father and mother leave me, the Lord will take me in.

Psalm 27:10

This is my command: Love each other as I have loved you. The greatest love a person can show is to die for his friends. You are my friends if you do what I command you.

John 15:12-14

I will not leave you all alone like orphans; I will come back to you.

John 14:18

God's love will continue forever.

Psalm 52:1

Jesus Is Your Family

Now you who are not Jewish are not foreigners or strangers any longer, but are citizens together with God's holy people. You belong to God's family.

Ephesians 2:19

My true brother and sister and mother are those who do what my Father in heaven wants.

Matthew 12:50

Jesus, who makes people holy, and those who are made holy are from the same family. So he is not ashamed to call them his brothers and sisters.

Hebrews 2:11

You were all baptized into Christ, and so you were all clothed with Christ. This means that you are all children of God through faith in Christ Jesus.

Galatians 3:26–27

But to all who did accept him and believe in him he gave the right to become children of God.

John 1:12

The Father has loved us so much that we are called children of God. And we really are his children. The reason the people in the world do not know us is that they have not known him.

1 John 3:1

Since you are God's children, God sent the Spirit of his Son into your hearts, and the Spirit cries out, "Father." So now you are not a slave; you are God's child, and God will give you the blessing he promised, because you are his child.

Galatians 4:6-7

The true children of God are those who let God's Spirit lead them.

Romans 8:14

Dear friends, now we are children of God, and we have not yet been shown what we will be in the future. But we know that when Christ comes again, we will be like him, because we will see him as he really is.

1 John 3:2

Jesus Is Your Protector

When you pass through the waters, I will be with you. When you cross rivers, you will not drown. When you walk through fire, you will not be burned, nor will the flames hurt you.

Isaiah 43:2

But, Lord, you are my shield, my wonderful God who gives me courage.

Psalm 3:3

But the Lord is faithful and will give you strength and will protect you from the Evil One.

2 Thessalonians 3:3

If you listen carefully to all he says and do everything that I tell you, I will be an enemy to your enemies. I will fight all who fight against you.

Exodus 23:22

He protects those who are loyal to him, but evil people will be silenced in darkness. Power is not the key to success.

1 Samuel 2:9

You have been my protection, like a strong tower against my enemies.

Psalm 61:3

The Lord your God is with you; the mighty One will save you. He will rejoice over you. You will rest in his love; he will sing and be joyful about you.

Zephaniah 3:17

The Lord sees the good people and listens to their prayers. But the Lord is against those who do evil. If you are trying hard to do good, no one can really hurt you.

1 Peter 3:12-13

At your side one thousand people may die, or even ten thousand right beside you, but you will not be hurt.

Psalm 91:7

Jesus Is Your Sure Thing

Jesus Christ is the same yesterday, today, and forever.

Hebrews 13:8

Now we hope for the blessings God has for his children. These blessings, which cannot be destroyed or be spoiled or lose their beauty, are kept in heaven for you.

1 Peter 1:4

My sheep listen to my voice; I know them, and they follow me. I give them eternal life, and they will never die, and no one can steal them out of my hand. My Father gave my sheep to me. He is greater than all, and no person can steal my sheep out of my Father's hand. The Father and I are one.

John 10:27-30

Look up to the skies. Who created all these stars? He leads out the army of heaven one by one and calls all the stars by name. Because he is strong and powerful, not one of them is missing.

Isaiah 40:26

God began doing a good work in you, and I am sure he will continue it until it is finished when Jesus Christ comes again.

Philippians 1:6

The Father gives me my people. Every one of them will come to me, and I will always accept them.

John 6:37

God has said, "I will never leave you; I will never forget you."

Hebrews 13:5

Surely your goodness and love will be with me all my life, and I will live in the house of the Lord forever.

Psalm 23:6

God gave you the Spirit to show that God will make you free when the final day comes.

Ephesians 4:30

These two things cannot change: God cannot lie when he makes a promise, and he cannot lie when he makes an oath. These things encourage us who came to God for safety. They give us strength to hold on to the hope we have been given. We have this hope as an anchor for the soul, sure and strong.

Hebrews 6:18-19

Jesus Is Your Answer

So I tell you to believe that you have received the things you ask for in prayer, and God will give them to you.

Mark 11:24

And God can give you more blessings than you need. Then you will always have plenty of everything—enough to give to every good work.

2 Corinthians 9:8

Serve him completely and willingly, because the Lord knows what is in everyone's mind. He understands everything you think. If you go to him for help, you will get an answer.

1 Chronicles 28:9

I know how to live when I am poor, and I know how to live when I have plenty. I have learned the secret of being happy at any time in everything that happens, when I have enough to eat and when I go hungry, when I have more than I need and when I do not have enough. I can do all things through Christ, because he gives me strength.

Philippians 4:12-13

And you will know that God's power is very great for us who believe. That power is the same as the great strength God used to raise Christ from the dead and put him at his right side in the heavenly world.

Ephesians 1:19-20

But he said to me, "My grace is enough for you. When your are weak, my power is made perfect in you." So I am very happy to brag about my weaknesses. Then Christ's power can live in me.

2 Corinthians 12:9

Praise be to the God and Father of our Lord Jesus Christ. In Christ, God has given us every spiritual blessing in the heavenly world.

Ephesians 1:3

If you remain in me and follow my teachings, you can ask anything you want, and it will be given to you.

John 15:7

Jesus Is Your EVERYTHING!

The church is filled with Christ, and Christ fills everything in every way.

Ephesians 1:23

My God will use his wonderful riches in Christ Jesus to give you everything you need.

Philippians 4:19

I can do all things through Christ, because he gives me strength.

Philippians 4:13

But in all these things we have full victory through God who showed his love for us.

Romans 8:37

With God's power working in us, God can do much, much more than anything we can ask or imagine. To him be glory in the church and in Christ Jesus for all time, forever and ever. Amen.

Ephesians 3:20-21

All that the Father has is mine. That is why I said that the Spirit will take what I have to say and tell it to you. In that day you will not ask me for anything. I tell you the truth, my Father will give you anything you ask for in my name.

John 16:15, 23

Praise be to the God and Father of our Lord Jesus Christ. In Christ, God has given us every spiritual blessing in the heavenly world.

Ephesians 1:3

And God gives us what we ask for because we obey God's commands and do what pleases him. This is what God commands: that we believe in his Son, Jesus Christ, and that we love each other, just as he commanded.

1 John 3:22-23

To me the only important thing about living is Christ, and dying would be profit for me.

Philippians 1:21

Jesus
Wants To . . .

Jesus Wants
To Fill You Up

Those who want to do right more than anything else are happy, because God will fully satisfy them.

Matthew 5:6

Enjoy serving the Lord, and he will give you what you want. Depend on the Lord; trust him, and he will take care of you.

Psalm 37:4–5

He satisfies the thirsty and fills up the hungry.

Psalm 107:9

He satisfies me with good things and makes me young again, like the eagle.

Psalm 103:5

Then Jesus said, "I am the bread that gives life. Whoever comes to me will never be hungry, and whoever believes in me will never be thirsty."

John 6:35

If you feed those who are hungry and take care of the needs of those who are troubled, then your light will shine in the darkness, and you will be bright like sunshine at noon. The Lord will always lead you. He will satisfy your needs in dry lands and give strength to your bones. You will be like a garden that has much water, like a spring that never runs dry.

Isaiah 58:10–11

All living things look to you for food, and you give it to them at the right time. You open your hand, and you satisfy all living things.

Psalm 145:15–16

Why spend your money on something that is not real food? Why work for something that doesn't really satisfy you? Listen closely to me, and you will eat what is good; your soul will enjoy the rich food that satisfies.

Isaiah 55:2

He did not spare his own Son but gave him for us all. So with Jesus, God will surely give us all things.

Romans 8:32

Jesus Wants To
Hang Out With You

Jesus answered, "If people love me, they will obey my teaching. My Father will love them, and we will come to them and make our home with them."

John 14:23

"Shout and be glad, Jerusalem. I am coming, and I will live among you," says the Lord.

Zechariah 2:10

We announce to you what we have seen and heard, because we want you also to have fellowship with us. Our fellowship is with God the Father and with his Son, Jesus Christ.

1 John 1:3

Here I am! I stand at the door and knock. If you hear my voice and open the door, I will come in and eat with you, and you will eat with me.

Revelation 3:20

This is true because if two or three people come together in my name, I am there with them.

Matthew 18:20

Those who know my commands and obey them are the ones who love me, and my Father will love those who love me. I will love them and will show myself to them.

John 14:21

Remain in me, and I will remain in you. A branch cannot produce fruit alone but must remain in the vine. In the same way, you cannot produce fruit alone but must remain in me. I am the vine, and you are the branches. If any remain in me and I remain in them, they produce much fruit. But without me they can do nothing. If you remain in me and follow my teachings, you can ask anything you want, and it will be given to you.

John 15:4–5, 7

Here is the message we have heard from Christ and now announced to you: God is light, and in him there is no darkness at all. So if we say we have fellowship with God, but we continue living in darkness, we are liars and do not follow the truth. But if we live in the light, as God is in the light, we can share fellowship with each other. Then the blood of Jesus, God's Son, cleanses us from every sin.

1 John 1:5–7

Jesus Wants
To Make You Holy

Because of God you are in Christ Jesus, who has become for us wisdom from God. In Christ we are put right with God, and have been made holy, and have been set free from sin.

1 Corinthians 1:30

Christ had no sin, but God made him become sin so that in Christ we could become right with God.

2 Corinthians 5:21

The Scriptures say the same thing about Abraham: "Abraham believed God, and God accepted Abraham's faith, and that faith made him right with God." So you should know that the true children of Abraham are those who have faith.

Galatians 3:6-7

But be holy in all you do, just as God, the One who called you, is holy. It is written in the Scriptures: "You must be holy, because I am holy."

1 Peter 1:15-16

God makes people right with himself through their faith in Jesus Christ. This is true for all who believe in Christ, because all people are the same.

Romans 3:22

All have sinned and are not good enough for God's glory, and all need to be made right with God by his grace, which is a free gift. They need to be made free from sin through Jesus Christ.

Romans 3:23–24

But people cannot do any work that will make them right with God. So they must trust in him, who makes even evil people right in his sight. Then God accepts their faith, and that makes them right with him.

Romans 4:5

But when the kindness and love of God our Savior was shown, he saved us because of his mercy. It was not because of good deeds we did to be right with him. He saved us through the washing that made us new people through the Holy Spirit.

Titus 3:44

We believe with our hearts, and so we are made right with God. And we use our mouths to say that we believe, and so we are saved.

Romans 10:10

Jesus Wants To Teach You About Forgiveness

But if we confess our sins, he will forgive our sins, because we can trust God to do what is right. He will cleanse us from all the wrongs we have done.

1 John 1:9

If anyone belongs to Christ, there is a new creation. The old things have gone; everything is made new!

2 Corinthians 5:17

He has taken our sins away from us as far as the east is from west.

Psalm 103:12

My dear children, I write this letter to you so you will not sin. But if anyone does sin, we have a helper in the presence of the Father—Jesus Christ, the one who does what is right.

1 John 2:1

In Christ we are set free by the blood of his death, and so we have forgiveness of sins. How rich is God's grace, which he has given to us so fully and freely.

Ephesians 1:7–8

I, I am the One who forgives all your sins, for my sake; I will not remember your sins.

Isaiah 43:25

I will forgive them for the wicked things they did, and I will not remember their sins anymore.

Hebrews 8:12

The wicked should stop doing wrong, and they should stop their evil thoughts. They should return to the Lord so he may have mercy on them. They should come to our God, because he will freely forgive them.

Isaiah 55:7

Get along with each other, and forgive each other. If someone does wrong to you, forgive that person because the Lord forgave you.

Colossians 3:13

When you are praying, if you are angry with someone, forgive him so that your Father in heaven will also forgive your sins.

Mark 11:25

When you were spiritually dead because of your sins and because you were not free from the power of your sinful self, God made you alive with Christ, and he forgave all our sins.

Colossians 2:13

The Lord says, "Come, let us talk about these things. Though your sins are like scarlet, they can be as white as snow. Though your sins are deep red, they can be white like wool."

Isaiah 1:18

Happy is the person whose sins are forgiven.

Psalm 32:1

What To
Do When
You Feel . . .

What To Do When You Feel Discouraged

We have troubles all around us, but we are not defeated. We do not know what to do, but we do not give up the hope of living. We are persecuted, but God does not leave us. We are hurt sometimes, but we are not destroyed.

2 Corinthians 4:8–9

The people the Lord has freed will return and enter Jerusalem with joy. Their happiness will last forever. They will have joy and gladness, and all sadness and sorrow will be gone far away.

Isaiah 51:11

Lord, even when I have trouble all around me, you will keep me alive. When my enemies are angry, you will reach down and save me by your power.

Psalm 138:7

Jesus said, "Don't let your hearts be troubled. Trust in God, and trust in me."

John 14:1

I leave you peace; my peace I
give you. I do not give it to you
as the world does. So don't let
your hearts be troubled or afraid.

John 14:27

So do not lose the courage you had in the past,
which has a great reward. You must hold on, so you
can do what God wants and receive what he has
promised.

Hebrews 10:35–36

God began doing a good work in you, and I am
sure he will continue it until it is finished when Jesus
Christ comes again.

Philippians 1:6

We must not become tired of doing good. We will
receive our harvest of eternal life at the right time if
we do not give up.

Galatians 6:9

All you who put your hope in the Lord be strong
and brave.

Psalm 31:24

The Lord is my light and the one who saves me. I

fear no one. The Lord protects my life; I am afraid of no one. Evil people may try to destroy my body. My enemies and those who hate me attack me, but they are overwhelmed and defeated. If an army surrounds me, I will not be afraid. If war breaks out, I will trust the Lord.

Psalm 27:1-3

The Lord is close to the brokenhearted, and he saves those whose spirits have been crushed.

Psalm 34:18

What To Do When You Feel Worried

Give all your worries to him, because he cares about you.

1 Peter 5:7

Do not worry about anything, but pray and ask God for everything you need, always giving thanks. And God's peace, which is so great we cannot understand it, will keep your hearts and minds in Christ Jesus.

Philippians 4:6-7

Let the peace that Christ gives control your thinking, because you were all called together in one body to have peace. Always be thankful.

Colossians 3:15

So don't worry, because I am with you. Don't be afraid, because I am your God. I will make you strong and will help you; I will support you with my right hand that saves you.

Isaiah 41:10

You, Lord, give true peace to those who depend on you, because they trust you.

Isaiah 26:3

So I tell you, don't worry about the food or drink you need to live, or about the clothes you need for your body. Life is more than food, and the body is more than clothes. Look at the birds in the air. They don't plant or harvest or store food in barns, but your heavenly Father feeds them. And you know that you are worth much more than the birds. You cannot add any time to your life by worrying about it.

Matthew 6:27

Don't have so little faith! Don't worry and say, 'What will we eat?' or 'What will we drink?' or 'What will we wear?' The people who don't know God keep trying to get these things, and your Father in heaven knows you need them. The thing you should want most is God's kingdom and doing what God wants. Then all these other things you need will be given to you. So don't worry about tomorrow, because tomorrow will have its own worries. Each day has enough trouble of its own.

Matthew 6:30–34

If people's thinking is controlled by the sinful self, there is death. But if their thinking is controlled by the Spirit, there is life and peace.

Romans 8:6

Those who love your teachings will find true peace, and nothing will defeat them.

Psalm 119:165

[Jesus said] I leave you peace; my peace I give you. I do not give it to you as the world does. So don't let your hearts be troubled or afraid.

John 14:27

But he said to me, "My grace is enough for you. When you are weak, my power is made perfect in you." So I am very happy to brag about my weaknesses. Then Christ's power can live in me.

2 Corinthians 12:9

What To Do When
You Feel Lonely

Teach them to obey everything that I have taught you, and I will be with you always, even until the end of this age.

Matthew 28:20

For his own sake, the Lord won't leave his people. Instead, he was pleased to make you his own people.

1 Samuel 12:22

[Jesus said] I will not leave you all alone like orphans; I will come back to you.

John 14:18

Jesus said, "Don't let your hearts be troubled. Trust in God, and trust in me."

John 14:1

Because the Lord your God is a merciful God. He will not leave you or destroy you. He will not forget the Agreement with your ancestors, which he swore to them.

Deuteronomy 4:31

The everlasting God is your place of safety, and his arms will hold you up forever.

Deuteronomy 33:27

He heals the broken hearted and bandages their wounds.

Psalm 147:3

Can anything separate us from the love Christ has for us? Can troubles or problems or sufferings or hunger or nakedness or danger or violent death? As it is written in the Scriptures: "For you we are in danger of death all the time. People think we are worth no more than sheep to be killed." But in all these things we have full victory through God who showed his love for us. Yes, I am sure that neither death, nor life, nor angels, nor ruling spirits, nothing now, nothing in the future, no powers, nothing above us, nothing below us, nor anything else in the whole world will ever be able to separate us from the love of God that is in Christ Jesus our Lord.

Romans 8:35-39

"The mountains may disappear, and the hills may come to an end, but my love will never disappear; my promise of peace will not come to an end," says the Lord who shows mercy to you.

Isaiah 54:10

Be strong and brave. Don't be afraid of them and don't be frightened, because the Lord your God will go with you. He will not leave you or forget you.

Deuteronomy 31:6

[Jesus said] I will be with you always, even until the end of this age.

Matthew 28:20

What To Do When You Feel Depressed

When you pass through the waters, I will be with you. When you cross rivers, you will not drown. When you walk through fire, you will not be burned, nor will the flames hurt you.

Isaiah 43:2

Crying may last for a night, but joy comes in the morning.

Psalm 30:5

My friends, do not be surprised at the terrible trouble which now comes to test you. Do not think that something strange is happening to you. But be happy that you are sharing in Christ's sufferings so that you will be happy and full of joy when Christ comes again in glory.

1 Peter 4:12–13

I will give them a crown to replace their ashes, and the oil of gladness to replace their sorrow, and clothes of praise to replace their spirit of sadness. Then they will be called Trees of Goodness, trees planted by the Lord to show his greatness.

Isaiah 61:3

But the people who trust the Lord will become strong again. They will rise up as an eagle in the sky; they will run and not need rest; they will walk and not become tired.

Isaiah 40:31

Praise be to the God and Father of our Lord Jesus Christ. God is the Father who is full of mercy and all comfort. He comforts us every time we have trouble, so when others have trouble, we can comfort them with the same comfort God gives us.

2 Corinthians 1:3-4

Yes, I am sure that neither death, nor life, not angels, nor ruling spirits, nothing now, nothing in the future, no powers, nothing above us, nothing below us, nor anything else in the whole world will ever be able to separate us from the love of God that is in Christ Jesus our Lord.

Romans 8:38-39

Brothers and sisters, think about the things that are good and worthy of praise. Think about the things that are true and honorable and right and pure and beautiful and respected.

Philippians 4:8

So don't worry, because I am with you. Don't be afraid, because I am your God. I will make you strong and will help you; I will support you with my right hand that saves you.

Isaiah 41:10

Be humble under God's powerful hand so he will lift you up when the right time comes. Give all your worries to him, because he cares about you.

1 Peter 5:6-7

Then Jesus used this story to teach his followers that they should always pray and never lose hope.

Luke 18:1

Nehemiah said, "Go and enjoy good food and sweet drinks. Send some to people who have none, because today is a holy day to the Lord. Don't be sad, because the joy of the Lord will make you strong."

Nehemiah 8:10

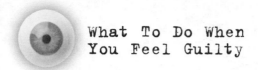

What To Do When You Feel Guilty

So now, those who are in Christ Jesus are not judged guilty.

Romans 8:1

He has not punished us as our sins should be punished; he has not repaid us for the evil we have done. He has taken our sins away from us as far as the east is from west.

Psalm 103:10, 12

God did not send his Son into the world to judge the world guilty, but to save the world through him. People who believe in God's Son are not judged guilty. Those who do not believe have already been judged guilty, because they have not believed in God's one and only Son.

John 3:17–18

[Jesus said] I tell you the truth, whoever hears what I say and believes in the One who sent me has eternal life. That person will not be judged guilty but has already left death and entered life.

John 5:24

Then I confessed my sins to you and didn't hide my guilt. I said, "I will confess my sins to the Lord," and you forgave my guilt.

Psalm 32:5

I will **forgive** them for the wicked things they did, and I will **not** remember their **sins** anymore.

Hebrews 8:12

But if we confess our sins, he will forgive our sins, because we can trust God to do what is right. He will cleanse us from all the wrongs we have done.

1 John 1:9

Jesus raised up again and asked her, "Woman, where are they? Has no one judged you guilty?" She answered, "No one, sir." Then Jesus said, "I also don't judge you guilty. You may go now, but don't sin anymore."

John 8:10-11

Let us come near to God with a sincere heart and a sure faith, because we have been made free from a guilty conscience, and our bodies have been washed with pure water.

Hebrews 10:22

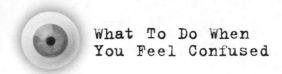

What To Do When You Feel Confused

God is **not a God of** confusion
but a God of **peace.**
1 Corinthians 14:33

God did not give us a spirit that makes us afraid but a spirit of power and love and self-control.

2 Timothy 1:7

Where jealousy and selfishness are, there will be confusion and every kind of evil. But the wisdom that comes from God is first of all pure, then peaceful, gentle, and easy to please. This wisdom is always ready to help those who are troubled and to do good for others. It is always fair and honest. People who work for peace in a peaceful way plant a good crop of right-living.

James 3:16-18

The Lord God helps me, so I will not be ashamed. I will be determined, and I know I will not be disgraced.

Isaiah 50:7

But if any of you needs wisdom, you should ask

God for it. He is generous and enjoys giving to all people, so he will give you wisdom.

James 1:5

Trust the Lord with all your heart, and don't depend on your own understanding. Remember the Lord in all you do, and he will give you success.

Proverbs 3:5–6

The Lord says, "I will make you wise and show you where to go. I will guide you and watch over you."

Psalm 32:8

If you go the wrong way—to the right or to the left—you will hear a voice behind you saying, "This is the right way. You should go this way."

Isaiah 30:21

Do not worry about anything, but pray and ask God for everything you need, always giving thanks. And God's peace, which is so great we cannot understand it, will keep your hearts and minds in Christ Jesus.

Philippians 4:6–7

What To Do When You Feel Tempted

If you think you are strong, you should be careful not to fall. The only temptation that has come to you is that which everyone has. But you can trust God, who will not permit you to be tempted more than you can stand. But when you are tempted, he will also give you a way to escape so that you will be able to stand it.

1 Corinthians 10:12–13

Since we have a great high priest, Jesus the Son of God, who has gone into heaven, let us hold on to the faith we have. For our high priest is able to understand our weaknesses. When he lived on earth, he was tempted in every way that we are, but he did not sin. Let us, then, feel very sure that we can come before God's throne where there is grace. There we can receive mercy and grace to help us when we need it.

Hebrews 4:14–16

And now he can help those who are tempted, because he himself suffered and was tempted.

Hebrews 2:18

So the Lord knows how to save those who serve him when troubles come.

2 Peter 2:9

Sin will not be your master, because you are not under law but under God's grace.

Romans 6:14

I have taken your words to heart so I would not sin against you.

Psalm 119:11

When people are tempted, they should not say, "God is tempting me." Evil cannot tempt God, and God himself does not tempt anyone. But people are tempted when their own evil desire leads them away and traps them.

James 1:13-14

If you hide your sins, you will not succeed. If you confess and reject them, you will receive mercy.

Proverbs 28:13

But if we confess our sins, he will forgive our sins, because we can trust God to do what is right. He will cleanse us from all the wrongs we have done.

1 John 1:9

Control yourselves and be careful! The devil, your enemy, goes around like a roaring lion looking for someone to eat. Refuse to give in to him, by standing strong in your faith. You know that your Christian family all over the world is having the same kinds of suffering.

1 Peter 5:8-9

Finally, be strong in the Lord and in his great power. Put on the full armor of God so that you can fight against the devil's evil tricks. And also use the shield of faith with which you can stop all the burning arrows of the Evil One.

Ephesians 6:10-11, 16

So give yourselves completely to God. Stand against the devil, and the devil will run from you.

James 4:7

My dear children, you belong to God and have defeated them; because God's Spirit, who is in you, is greater than the devil, who is in the world.

1 John 4:4

God is strong and can help you not to fall. He can bring you before his glory without any wrong in you and can give you great joy. He is the only God, the One who saves us. To him be glory, greatness, power, and authority through Jesus Christ our Lord for all time past, now, and forever. Amen.

Jude 24–25

This makes you very happy, even though now for a short time different kinds of troubles may make you sad. These troubles come to prove that your faith is pure. This purity of faith is worth more than gold, which can be proved to be pure by fire but will ruin. But the purity of your faith will bring you praise and glory and honor when Jesus Christ is shown to you.

1 Peter 1:6–7

What To Do When You Feel Angry

My dear brothers and sisters, always be willing to listen and slow to speak. Do not become angry easily, because anger will not help you live the right kind of life God wants.

James 1:19-20

When you are angry, do not sin, and be sure to stop being angry before the end of the day.

Ephesians 4:26

A gentle answer will calm a person's anger, but an unkind answer will cause more anger.

Proverbs 15:1

Patient people have great understanding, but people with quick tempers show their foolishness.

Proverbs 14:29

Patience is better than strength. Controlling your temper is better than capturing a city.

Proverbs 16:32

Don't become angry quickly, because getting angry is foolish.

Ecclesiastes 7:9

My friends, do not try to punish others when they wrong you, but wait for God to punish them with his anger. It is written: "I will punish those who do wrong; I will repay them," says the Lord.

Romans 12:19

If your enemy is hungry, feed him. If he is thirsty, give him a drink. Doing this will be like pouring burning coals on his head, and the Lord will reward you.

Proverbs 25:21-22

We know that God said, "I will punish those who do wrong; I will repay them. "And he also said, "The Lord will judge his people."

Hebrews 10:30

Do not be bitter or angry or mad. Never shout angrily or say things to hurt others. Never do anything evil. Be kind and loving to each other, and forgive each other just as God forgave you in Christ.

Ephesians 4:31-32

But I tell you, if you are angry with a brother or sister, you will be judged. If you say bad things to a brother or sister, you will be judged by the council. And if you call someone a fool, you will be in danger of the fire of hell. So when you offer your gift to God at the altar, and you remember that your brother or sister has something against you, leave your gift there at the altar. Go and make peace with that person, and then come and offer your gift.

Matthew 5:22–24

Wise people are careful and stay out of trouble, but fools are careless and quick to act. Someone with a quick temper does foolish things, but someone with understanding remains calm.

Proverbs 14:16–17

But now also put these things out of your life: anger, bad temper, doing or saying things to hurt others, and using evil words when you talk.

Colossians 3:8

Don't get angry. Don't be upset; it only leads to trouble.

Psalm 37:8

What To Do When You Feel Rebellious

Obey your leaders and act under their authority. They are watching over you, because they are responsible for your souls. Obey them so that they will do this work with joy, not sadness. It will not help you to make their work hard.

Hebrews 13:17

Disobedience is as bad as the sin of sorcery. Pride is as bad as the sin of worshiping idols.

1 Samuel 15:23

For the Lord's sake, yield to the people who have authority in this world: the king, who is the highest authority, and the leaders who are sent by him to punish those who do wrong and to praise those who do right. It is God's desire that by doing good you should stop foolish people from saying stupid things about you.

1 Peter 2:13-15

In your lives you must think and act like Christ Jesus. Christ himself was like God in everything. But he

did not think that being equal with God was something to be used for his own benefit. But he gave up
his place with God and made himself nothing.

Philippians 2:5-7

Even though Jesus was the Son of God, he learned
obedience by what he suffered.

Hebrews 5:8

In the same way, younger people should be willing
to be under older people. And all of you should be
very humble with each other.

1 Peter 5:5

Yield to obey each other because you respect Christ.

Ephesians 5:21

In the past you were full of darkness, but now you
are full of light in the Lord. So live like children who
belong to the light.

Ephesians 5:8

What To Do When
You Feel Rejected

God does not see the same way people see. People look at the outside of a person, but the Lord looks at the heart.

1 Samuel 16:7

But if you suffer because you are a Christian, do not be ashamed. Praise God because you wear that name.

1 Peter 4:16

Happy are those who don't listen to the wicked, who don't go where sinners go, who don't do what evil people do. They love the Lord's teachings, and they think about those teachings day and night. They are strong, like a tree planted by a river. The tree produces fruit in season, and its leaves don't die. Everything they do will succeed.

Psalm 1:1-3

Those who are treated badly for doing good are happy, because the kingdom of heaven belongs to them.

Matthew 5:10-12

The Father gives me my people. Every one of them will come to me, and I will always accept them.

John 6:37

Depend on the Lord; trust him, and he will take care of you. Then your goodness will shine like the sun, and your fairness like the noonday sun. Wait and trust the Lord. Don't be upset when others get rich or when someone else's plans succeed.

Psalm 37:5-7

God has chosen you and made you his holy people. He loves you. So always do these things: Show mercy to others, be kind, humble, gentle, and patient. Get along with each other, and forgive each other. If someone does wrong to you, forgive that person because the Lord forgave you. Do all these things; but most important, love each other. Love is what holds you all together in perfect unity.

Colossians 3:12-14

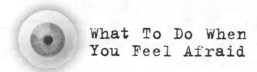

What To Do When You Feel Afraid

God did not give us a spirit that makes us afraid but a spirit of power and love and self-control.

2 Timothy 1:7

Where God's love is, there is no fear, because God's perfect love drives out fear.

1 John 4:18a

Those who go to God Most High for safety will be protected by the Almighty. I will say to the Lord, "You are my place of safety and protection. You are my God and I trust you."

Psalm 91:1-2

He will cover you with his feathers, and under his wings you can hide. His truth will be your shield and protection. You will not fear any danger by night or an arrow during the day.

Psalm 91:4-5

Nothing bad will happen to you; no disaster will come to your home. He has put his angels in charge of you to watch over you wherever you go. . . . The LORD says, "Whoever loves me, I will save. I will protect those who know me."

Psalm 91:10–11, 14

Even if I walk through a very dark valley, I will not be afraid, because you are with me.

Psalm 23:4

I trust in God. I will not be afraid. What can people do to me?

Psalm 56:11

If God is with us,
no one can defeat us.

Romans 8:29

All you who put your hope in the Lord be strong and brave.

Psalm 31:24

What To
Do When
You Are . . .

What To Do When You Are Dealing with Too Much Too Fast

Wait for the Lord's help. Be strong and brave, and wait for the Lord's help.

Psalm 27:14

The Lord is good to those who hope in him, to those who seek him. It is good to wait quietly for the Lord to save.

Lamentations 3:25-26

So do not lose the courage you had in the past, which has a great reward. You must hold on, so you can do what God wants and receive what he has promised.

Hebrews 10:35-36

We ask you, brothers and sisters, to warn those who do not work. Encourage the people who are afraid. Help those who are weak. Be patient with everyone.

1 Thessalonians 5:14

Wait and trust the Lord. Don't be upset when others get rich or when someone else's plans succeed. Don't get angry. Don't be upset; it only leads to trouble. It is better to have little and be right than to have much and be wrong.

Psalm 37:7-8, 16

I waited patiently for the Lord. He turned to me and heard my cry.

Psalm 40:1

We also have joy with our troubles, because we know that these troubles produce patience. And patience produces character, and character produces hope. And this hope will never disappoint us, because God has poured out his love to fill our hearts. He gave us his love through the Holy Spirit, whom God has given to us.

Romans 5:3-5

My brothers and sisters, when you have many kinds of troubles, you should be full of joy, because you now that these troubles test your faith, and this will give you patience. Let your patience show itself perfectly in what you do. Then you will be perfect and complete and will have everything you need.

James 1:2-4

Brothers and sisters, be patient until the Lord comes again. A farmer patiently waits for his valuable crop to grow from the earth and for it to receive the autumn and spring rains. You, too, must be patient. Do not give up hope, because the Lord is coming soon.

James 5:7-8

What To Do When
You Are Bummed Out

You, Lord, give true peace to those who depend on you, because they trust you. So, trust the Lord always, because he is our rock forever.

Isaiah 26:3-4

The Lord God will wipe away every tear from every face. He will take away the shame of his people from the earth. The Lord has spoken. At that time people will say, "Our God is doing this! We have waited for him, and he has come to save us. This is the Lord. We waited for him, so we will rejoice and be happy when he saves us."

Isaiah 25:8-9

The Lord says, "My thoughts are not like your thoughts. Your ways are not like my ways. Just as the heavens are higher than the earth, so are my ways higher than your ways and my thoughts higher than your thoughts. So you will go out with joy and be led out in peace. The mountains and hills will burst into song before you, and all the trees in the fields will clap their hands."

Isaiah 55:8-9, 12

The Lord saves good people; he is their strength in times of trouble. The Lord helps them and saves them; he saves them from the wicked, because they trust in him for protection.

Psalm 37:39–40

Those who love your teachings will find true peace, and nothing will defeat them. I am waiting for you to save me, Lord. I will obey your commands. I obey your rules, and I love them very much. I obey your orders and rules, because you know everything I do. Hear my cry to you, Lord. Let your word help me understand.

Psalm 119:165–169

"I will give peace, real peace, to those far and near, and I will heal them," says the Lord. But evil people are like the angry sea, which cannot rest, whose waves toss up waste and mud. "There is no peace for evil people," says my God.

Isaiah 57:19–21

The power of the wicked will be broken, but the Lord supports those who do right. The Lord watches over the lives of the innocent, and their reward will last forever. They will not be ashamed when trouble comes. They will be full in times of hunger.

Psalm 37:17–19

God once said, "Let the light shine out of the darkness!" This is the same God who made his light shine in our hearts by letting us know the glory of God that is in the face of Christ. We have troubles all around us, but we are not defeated. We do not know what to do, but we do not give up the hope of living. We are persecuted, but God does not leave us. We are hurt sometimes, but we are not destroyed.

2 Corinthians 4:6, 8-9

What To Do When You Are Flirting with Sin

Wake up! Make yourselves stronger before what you have left dies completely. I have found that what you are doing is less than what my God wants. I know what you do, that you are not hot or cold! But because you are lukewarm—neither hot, nor cold—I am ready to spit you out of my mouth. I correct and punish those whom I love. So be eager to do right, and change your hearts and lives.

Revelation 3:2, 15-16, 19

But I have this against you: You have left the love you had in the beginning. So remember where you were before you fell. Change your hearts and do what you did at first. If you do not change, I will come to you and will take away your lampstand from its place.

Revelation 2:4-5

Come back to the Lord and say these words to him: "Take away all our sin and kindly receive us, and we will keep the promises we made to you." . . . The Lord says, "I will forgive them for leaving me and will love them freely, because I am not angry with them anymore."

Hosea 14:2, 4

Do not change yourselves to be like the people of this world, but be changed within by a new way of thinking. Then you will be able to decide what God wants for you; you will know what is good and pleasing to him and what is perfect.

Romans 12:2

Innocent people will be kept safe, but those who are dishonest will suddenly be ruined.

Proverbs 28:18

The honest person will live in safety, but the dishonest will be caught. The words of a good person give life, like a fountain of water, but the words of the wicked contain nothing but violence.

Proverbs 10:9, 11

Know in your heart that the Lord your God corrects you as a parent corrects a child. Obey the commands of the Lord your God, living as he has commanded you and respecting him.

Deuteronomy 8:5-6

So brothers and sisters, be careful that none of you has an evil, unbelieving heart that will turn you away from the living God. But encourage each other every day while it is "today." Help each other so none of you will become hardened because sin has tricked you.

Hebrews 5:11-12

They were made free from the evil in the world by knowing our Lord and Savior Jesus Christ. But if they return to evil things and those things control them, then it is worse for them than it was before. Yes, it would be better for them to have never known the right way than to know it and to turn away from the holy teaching that was given to them.

2 Peter 2:20-21

What To Do When You Are Uncertain About God

Jesus answered, "Have faith in God. I tell you the truth, you can say to this mountain, 'Go, fall into the sea.' And if you have no doubts in your mind and believe that what you say will happen, God will do it for you. So I tell you to believe that you have received the things you ask for in prayer, and God will give them to you. When you are praying, if you are angry with someone, forgive him so that your Father in heaven will also forgive your sins."

Mark 11:22–25

Abraham was almost a hundred years old, much past the age for having children, and Sarah could not have children. Abraham thought about all this, but his faith in God did not become weak.

Romans 4:19–21

Now may God himself, the God of peace, make you pure, belonging only to him. May your whole self—spirit, soul, and body—be kept safe and without fault when our Lord Jesus Christ comes. You can trust the One who calls you to do that for you.

1 Thessalonians 5:23–24

The Lord is not slow in doing what he promised the way some people understand slowness. But God is being patient with you. He does not want anyone to be lost, but he wants all people to change their hearts and lives.

2 Peter 3:9

The ways of God are without fault. The Lord's words are pure. He is a shield to those who trust him. Who is God? Only the Lord. Who is the Rock? Only our God. God is my protection. He makes my way free from fault.

Psalm 18:30-32

So faith comes from hearing the Good News, and people hear the Good News when someone tells them about Christ.

Romans 10:17

Rain and snow fall from the sky and don't return without watering the ground. They cause the plants to sprout and grow, making seeds for the farmer and bread for the people. The same thing is true of the words I speak. They will not return to me empty. They make the things happen that I want to happen, and they succeed in doing what I send them to do.

Isaiah 55:10-11

What To
Do When . . .

What To Do When You Don't Feel Important

So do not lose the courage you had in the past, which has a great reward. You must hold on, so you can do what God wants and receive what he has promised.

Hebrews 10:35-36

God began doing a good work in you, and I am sure he will continue it until it is finished when Jesus Christ comes again.

Philippians 1:6

And I pray that you and all God's holy people will have the power to understand the greatness of Christ's love—how wide and how long and how high and how deep that love is. Christ's love is greater than anyone can ever know, but I pray that you will be able to know that love. Then you can be filled with the fullness of God.

Ephesians 3:18-19

You were taught to leave your old self—to stop living the evil way you lived before. That old self becomes worse, because people are fooled by evil things they want to do. But you were taught to be made new in your hearts.

Ephesians 4:22-23

Also, the Spirit helps us with our weakness. We do not know how to pray as we should. But the Spirit himself speaks to God for us, even begs God for us with deep feelings that words cannot explain. God can see what is in the mind of the Spirit, because the Spirit speaks to God for his people in the way God wants.

Romans 8:26-27

But the people who trust the Lord will become strong again. They will rise up as an eagle in the sky; they will run and not need rest; they will walk and not become tired.

Isaiah 40:31

When our hearts make us feel guilty, we can still have peace before God. God is greater than our hearts, and he knows everything.

1 John 3:20

Those who believe will do even greater things than these, because I am going to the Father.

John 14:12

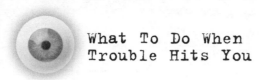

What To Do When Trouble Hits You

The Lord is good, giving protection in times of trouble. He knows who trusts in him.

Nahum 1:7

Jesus said, "Don't let your hearts be troubled.
Trust in God, and trust in me."

John 14:1

We know that in everything God works for the good of those who love him. They are the people he called, because that was his plan.

Romans 8:28

I will be glad and rejoice in your love, because you saw my suffering; you knew my troubles.

Psalm 31:7

I look up to the hills, but where does my help come from? My help comes from the Lord, who made heaven and earth.

Psalm 121:1-2

Praise be to the God and Father of our Lord Jesus Christ. God is the Father who is full of mercy and all comfort. He comforts us every time we have trouble, so when others have trouble, we can comfort them with the same comfort God gives us.

2 Corinthians 1:3-4

Do not worry about anything, but pray and ask God for everything you need, always giving thanks. And God's peace, which is so great we cannot understand it, will keep your hearts and minds in Christ Jesus.

Philippians 4:6-7

My brothers and sisters, when you have many kinds of troubles, you should be full of joy, because you know that these troubles test your faith, and this will give you patience. When people are tempted and still continue strong, they should be happy. After they have proved their faith, God will reward them with life forever. God promised this to all those who love him.

James 1:2-3, 12

What To Do When You Are Sick

My dear friend, I know your soul is doing fine, and I pray that you are doing well in every way and that your health is good.

3 John 2

Jesus traveled through all the towns and villages, teaching in their synagogues, preaching the Good News about the kingdom, and healing all kinds of diseases and sicknesses.

Matthew 9:35

All the people were trying to touch Jesus, because power was coming from him and healing them all.

Luke 6:19

Christ carried our sins in his body on the cross so we would stop living for sin and start living for what is right. And you are healed because of his wounds.

1 Peter 2:24

Anyone who is sick should call the church's elders. They should pray for and pour oil on the person in the name of the Lord. And the prayer that is said with faith will make the sick person well; the Lord will heal that person. And if the person has sinned, the sins will be forgiven.

James 5:14–15

But he was wounded for the wrong we did; he was crushed for the evil we did. The punishment, which made us well, was given to him, and we are healed because of his wounds.

Isaiah 53:5

Lord, heal me, and I will truly be healed. Save me, and I will truly be saved. You are the one I praise.

Jeremiah 17:14

"I will bring back your health and heal your injuries," says the Lord.

Jeremiah 30:17

My child, pay attention to my words; listen closely to what I say. Don't ever forget my words; keep them always in mind. They are the key to life for those who find them; they bring health to the whole body.

Proverbs 4:20–22

God gave the command and healed them, so they were saved from dying.

Psalm 107:20

The officer answered, "Lord, I am not worthy for you to come into my house. You only need to command it, and my servant will be healed."

Matthew 8:8

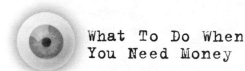

What To Do When You Need Money

When a person's steps follow the Lord, God is pleased with his ways. If he stumbles, he will not fall, because the Lord holds his hand. I was young, and now I am old, but I have never seen good people left helpless or their children begging for food.

Psalm 37:23-25

Even lions may get weak and hungry, but those who look to the Lord will have every good thing.

Psalm 34:10

The Lord is my shepherd; I have everything I need.

Psalm 23:1

The Lord your God is bringing you into a good land, a land with rivers and pools of water, with springs that flow in the valleys and hills, a land that has wheat and barley, vines, fig trees, pomegranates, olive oil, and honey. It is a land where you will have plenty of food, where you will have everything you need, where the rocks are iron, and where you can dig copper out of the hills. When you have all you want to eat, then praise the Lord your God for giving you a good land. Be careful not to forget the Lord your God so that you fail to obey his commands, laws, and rules that I am giving to you today.

Deuteronomy 8:7-14

Don't worry and say, "What will we eat?" or "What will we drink?" or "What will we wear?" The people who don't know God keep trying to get these things, and your Father in heaven knows you need them. The thing you should want most is God's kingdom and doing what God wants. Then all these other things you need will be given to you.

Matthew 6:31-33

Those who want to become rich bring temptation to themselves and are caught in a trap. They want many foolish and harmful things that ruin and destroy people. The love of money causes all kinds of evil. Some people have left the faith, because they wanted to get more money, but they have caused themselves much sorrow.

1 Timothy 6:9-10

The earth belongs to the Lord, and everything in it—the world and all its people.

Psalm 24:1

Give, and you will receive. You will be given much. Pressed down, shaken together, and running over, it will spill into your lap. The way you give to others is the way God will give to you.

Luke 6:38

On the first day of every week, each one of you should put aside money as you have been blessed.

1 Corinthians 16:2

"Bring to the storehouse a full tenth of what you earn so there will be food in my house. Test me this," says the Lord All–Powerful. "I will open the windows of heaven for you and pour out all the blessings you need. I will stop the insects so they won't eat your crops. The grapes won't fall from your vines before they are ready to pick," says the Lord All–Powerful.

Malachi 3:10–11

Remember this: The person who plants a little will have a small harvest, but the person who plants a lot will have a big harvest. Each one of you should give as you have decided in your heart to give. You should not be sad when you give, and you should not give because you feel forced to give. God loves the person who gives happily. And God can give you more blessings than you need. Then you will always have plenty of everything—enough to give to every good work.

2 Corinthians 9:6–8

Good people leave their wealth to their grandchildren, but a sinner's wealth is stored up for good people.

Proverbs 13:22

No one can serve two masters. The person will hate one master and love the other, or will follow one master and refuse to follow the other. You cannot serve both God and worldly riches.

Matthew 6:24

What To Do When Someone Close to You Dies

Brothers and sisters, we want you to know about those Christians who have died so you will not be sad, as others who have no hope. We believe that Jesus died and that he rose again. So, because of him, God will raise with Jesus those who have died.

1 Thessalonians 4:13-14

The Lord comforts his people and will have pity on those who suffer.

Isaiah 49:13b

Those who are sad now are happy, because God will comfort them.

Matthew 5:4

He comforts us every time we have trouble, so when others have trouble, we can comfort them with the same comfort God gives us. We share in the many sufferings of Christ. In the same way, much comfort comes to us through Christ.

2 Corinthians 1:4-5

He will wipe away every tear from their eyes, and there will be no more death, sadness, crying, or pain, because all the old ways are gone.

Revelation 21:4

Lord, show me your love, and save me as you have promised. When I suffer, this comforts me: Your promise gives me life.

Psalm 119:41, 50

"Death, where is your victory? Death, where is your pain?" Death's power to hurt is sin, and the power of sin is the law. But we thank God! He gives us the victory through our Lord Jesus Christ.

1 Corinthians 15:55-57

So don't worry, because I am with you. Don't be afraid because I am your God. I will make you strong and will help you; I will support you with my right hand that saves you.

Isaiah 41:10

So I say that we have courage. We really want to be away from this body and be at home with the Lord.

Our only goal is to please God whether we live here or there, because we must all stand before Christ to be judged. Each of us will receive what we should get— good or bad—for the things we did in the earthly body.

2 Corinthians 5:8-10

What To Do When You Don't Understand God's Ways

The Lord says, "My thoughts are not like your thoughts. Your ways are not like my ways. Just as the heavens are higher than the earth, so are my ways higher than your ways and my thoughts higher than your thoughts."

Isaiah 55:8-9

Judah, pray to me, and I will answer you. I will tell you important secrets you have never heard before.

Jeremiah 33:3

The only temptation that has come to you is that which everyone has. But you can trust God, who will not permit you to be tempted more than you can stand. But when you are tempted, he will also give you a way to escape so that you will be able to stand it.

1 Corinthians 10:13

People who do what is right may have many problems, but the Lord will solve them all.

Psalm 34:19

My friends, do not be surprised at the terrible trouble which now comes to test you. Do not think that something strange is happening to you. But be happy that you are sharing in Christ's sufferings so that you will be happy and full of joy when Christ comes again in glory.

1 Peter 4:12-13

Come, let's go back to the Lord. He has hurt us, but he will heal us. He has wounded us, but he will bandage our wounds. In two days he will put new life in us; on the third day he will raise us up so that we may live in his presence and know him. Let's try to learn about the Lord; He will come to us as surely as the dawn comes. He will come to us like rain, like the spring rain that waters the ground.

Hosea 6:1-3

The ways of God are without fault. The Lord's words are pure. He is a shield to those who trust him.

Psalm 18:30

Let us hold firmly to the hope that we have confessed, because we can trust God to do what he promised.

Hebrews 10:23

What To Do When Nothing Seems to Be Going Right

But the people who trust the Lord will become strong again. They will rise up as an eagle in the sky; they will run and not need rest; they will walk and not become tired.

Isaiah 40:31

I find **rest** in God;
only he gives me **hope**.

Psalm 62:5

It is not yet time for the message to come true, but that time is coming soon; the message will come true. It may seem like a long time, but be patient and wait for it, because it will surely come; it will not be delayed.

Habakkuk 2:3

Let us hold firmly to the hope that we have confessed, because we can trust God to do what he promised.

Hebrews 10:23

I wait for the Lord to help me, and I trust his word.

Psalm 130:5

We all share in Christ if we keep till the end the sure faith we had in the beginning.

Hebrews 3:14

At that time people will say, "Our God is doing this! We have waited for him, and he has come to save us. This is the Lord. We waited for him, so we will rejoice and be happy when he saves us."

Isaiah 25:9

So be very careful how you live. Do not live like those who are not wise, but live wisely.

Ephesians 5:15

The
Bible Is . . .

The Bible Is
The Real Deal

All Scripture is given by God and is useful for teaching, for showing people what is wrong in their lives, for correcting faults, and for teaching how to live right. Using the Scriptures, the person who serves God will be capable, having all that is needed to do every good work.

2 Timothy 3:16-17

Most of all, you must understand this: No prophecy in the Scriptures ever comes from the prophet's own interpretation. No prophecy ever came from what a person wanted to say, but people led by the Holy Spirit spoke words from God.

2 Peter 1:20-21

God's word is alive and working and is sharper than a double-edged sword. It cuts all the way into us, where the soul and the spirit are joined, to the center of out joints and bones. And it judges the thoughts and feelings in our hearts. Nothing in all the world can be hidden from God. Everything is clear and lies open before him, and to him we must explain the way we have lived.

Hebrews 4:12-13

Rain and snow fall from the sky and don't return without watering the ground. They cause the plants to sprout and grow, making seeds for the farmer and bread for the people. The same thing is true of he words I speak. They will not return to me empty. They make the things that I want to happen, and they succeed in doing what I send them to do.

Isaiah 55:10-11

Earth and sky will be destroyed, but the words I have said will never be destroyed.

Mark 13:31

You have been born again, and this new life did not come from something that dies, but from something that cannot die. You were born again through God's living message that continues forever. The Scripture says, "All people are like the grass, and all their glory is like the flowers of the field. The grass dies and the flowers fall, but the word of the Lord will live forever." And this is the word that was preached to you.

1 Peter 1:23-23

Every word of God is true. He guards those who come to him for safety.

Proverbs 30:5

Lord, your word is everlasting; it continues forever in heaven.

Psalm 119:89

The yes to all of God's promises is in Christ, and through Christ we say yes to the glory of God.

2 Corinthians 1:20

The Bible Is
Your Extreme Strength

Now I am putting you in the care of God and the message about his grace. It is able to give you strength, and it will give you the blessings God has for all his holy people.

Acts 20:32

[Jesus said] Stand up! I have chosen you to be my servant and my witness—you will tell the people things that you have seen and the things that I will show you. This is why I have come to you today. I am sending you to them to open their eyes so that they may turn away from darkness to the light, away from the power of Satan and to God.

Acts 26:16-18

In Christ we were chosen to be God's people, because from the very beginning God had decided this in keeping with his plan. And he is the One who makes everything agree with what he decides and wants. We are the first people who hoped in Christ, and we were chosen so that we would bring praise to God's glory. So it is with you. When you heard the true teaching—the Good News about your salvation—you believed in Christ. And in Christ, God put his special mark of ownership on you by giving you the Holy Spirit he had promised for his people until God gives full freedom to those who are his—to bring praise to God's glory.

Ephesians 1:11-14

You belong to Christ, so you are Abraham's descendants. You will inherit all of God's blessings because of the promise God made to Abraham.

Galatians 3:29

This is that secret: that through the Good News those who are not Jews will share with the Jews in God's blessing. They belong to the same body, and they share together in the promise that God made in Christ Jesus.

Ephesians 3:6

But as it is written in the Scriptures: "No one has ever seen this, and no one has ever heard about it. No one has ever imagined what God has prepared for those who love him."

1 Corinthians 2:9

In all the work you are doing, work the best you can. Work as if you were doing it for the Lord, not for people. Remember that you will receive your reward from the Lord, which he promised to his people. You are serving the Lord Christ.

Colossians 3:23-24

The Bible Is Your
Locker of Truth

Your word is like a lamp for my feet and a light for my path.

Psalm 119:105

My son, keep your father's commands, and don't forget your mother's teaching. Keep their words in mind forever as though you had them tied around your neck. They will guide you when you walk. They will guard you when you sleep. They will speak to you when you are awake. These commands are like a lamp; this teaching is like a light. And the correction that comes from them will help you have life.

Proverbs 6:20–23

I have taken your words to heart so I would not sin against you.

Psalm 119:11

The orders of the Lord are right; they make people happy. The commands of the Lord are pure; they light up the way. Respect for the Lord is good; it will last forever. The judgments of the Lord are true; they are completely right. They are worth more than gold, even the purest gold. They are sweeter than honey, even the finest honey. By them your servant is warned. Keeping them brings great reward.

Psalm 19:8-11

How can a young person live a pure life? By obeying your word.

Psalm 119:9

So Jesus said to the Jews who believed in him, "If you continue to obey my teaching, you are truly my followers. Then you will know the truth, and the truth will make you free."

John 8:31-32

All Scripture is given by God and is useful for teaching, for showing people what is wrong in their lives, for correcting faults, and for teaching how to live right. Using the Scriptures, the person who serves God will be capable, having all that is needed to do every good work.

2 Timothy 3:16-17

Your rules give me pleasure; they give me good advice.

Psalm 119:24

The Lord says, "I will make you wise and show you where to go. I will guide you and watch over you."

Psalm 32:8

Always remember what is written in the Book of the Teachings. Study it day and night to be sure to obey everything that is written there. If you do this, you will be wise and successful in everything.

Joshua 1:8

The Bible Is the
Internet for Your Soul

That is why you need to put on God's full armor. Then on the day of evil you will be able to stand strong. And when you have finished the whole fight, you will still be standing. So stand strong, with the belt of truth tied around your waist and the protection of right living on your chest.

Ephesians 6:13-14

God will strengthen you with his own great power so that you will not give up when troubles come, but you will be patient. And you will joyfully give thanks to the Father who has made you able to have a share in all that he has prepared for his people in the kingdom of light.

Colossians 1:11-12

I ask the Father in his great glory to give you the power to be strong inwardly through his Spirit. I pray that Christ will live in your hearts by faith and that your life will be strong in love and be built on love.

Ephesians 3:16-17

I am sad and tired. Make me strong again as you have promised.

Psalm 119:28

Nehemiah said, "Go and enjoy good food and sweet drinks. Send some to people who have none, because today is a holy day to the Lord. Don't be sad, because the joy of the Lord will make you strong."

Nehemiah 8:10

I have good sense and advice, and I have understanding and power.

Proverbs 8:14

I love you, Lord. You are my strength. The Lord is my rock, my protection, my Savior. My God is my rock. I can run to him for safety. He is my shield and my saving strength, my defender. I will call to the Lord, who is worthy of praise, and I will be saved from my enemies.

Psalm 18:1–3

Finally, be strong in the Lord and in his great power.

Ephesians 6:10

Straight Talk
From God's
Word About . . .

Straight Talk From God's Word About Being Obedient

See, today I am letting you choose a blessing or a curse. You will be blessed if you obey the commands of the Lord your God that I am giving you today. But you will be cursed if you disobey the commands of the Lord your God.

Deuteronomy 11:26-28

Obey me, and I will be your God and you will be my people. Do all that I command so that good things will happen to you.

Jeremiah 7:23

If you love me, you will obey my commands. Those who know my commands and obey them are the ones who love me, and my Father will love those who love me. I will love them and will show myself to them.

John 14:15, 21

Peter and the other apostles answered, "We must obey God, not human authority!"

Acts 5:29

He is the way our sins are taken away, and not only our sins but the sins of all people. We can be sure that we know God if we obey his commands. Anyone who says, "I know God," but doesn't obey his commands is a liar, and the truth is not in that person. But if someone obeys God's teaching, then in that person God's love has truly reached its goal.

1 John 2:2-5

Children, obey your parents as the Lord wants, because this is the right thing to do.

Ephesians 6:1

Children, obey your parents in all things, because this pleases the Lord. . . . Do not obey just when they are watching you, to gain their favor, but serve them honestly, because you respect the Lord.

Colossians 3:20, 22

Straight Talk From God's Word About Sellin' Out to the World

You want things, but you do not have them. So you are ready to kill and are jealous of other people, but you still cannot get what you want. So you argue and fight. You do not get what you want, because you do not ask God. Or when you ask, you do not receive because the reason you ask is wrong. You want things so you can use them for your own pleasures. So, you are not loyal to God! You should know that loving the world is the same as hating God. Anyone who wants to be a friend of the world becomes God's enemy.

James 4:2–4

Some people think they are doing right, but in the end it leads to death. Someone who is laughing may be sad inside, and joy may end in sadness. Evil people will be paid back for their evil ways, and good people will be rewarded for their good ones.

Proverbs 14:12–14

Many people live like enemies of the cross of Christ. I have often told you about them, and it makes me cry to tell you about them now. In the end, they will be destroyed. They do whatever their bodies want, they are proud of their shameful acts, and they think only about earthly things. But our homeland is in heaven, and we are waiting for our Savior, the Lord Jesus Christ, to come from heaven. By his power to rule all things, he will change our simple bodies and make them like his own glorious body.

Philippians 3:18–21

If people's thinking is controlled by the sinful self, there is death. But if their thinking is controlled by the Spirit, there is life and peace.

Romans 8:6–8

Dear friends, you are like foreigners and strangers in this world. I beg you to avoid the evil things your bodies want to do that fight against your soul. People who do not believe are living all around you and might say that you are doing wrong. Live such good lives that they will see the good things you do and will give glory to God on the day when Christ comes again.

1 Peter 2:11–12

Do not love the world or the things in the world. If you love the world, the love of the Father is not in you.

These are the ways of the world: wanting to please our sinful selves, wanting the sinful things we see, and being too proud of what we have. None of these come from the Father, but all of them come from the world. The world and everything that people want in it are passing away, but the person who does what God wants lives forever.

1 John 2:15-17

Straight Talk From God's Word About Sex

God wants you to be holy and to stay away from sexual sins. He wants each of you to learn to control your own body in a way that is holy and honorable. Don't use your body for sexual sin like the people who do not know God.

1 Thessalonians 4:14

Surely you know that the people who do wrong will not inherit God's kingdom. Do not be fooled. Those who sin sexually, worship idols, take part in adultery, those who are male prostitutes, or men who have sexual relations with other men, those who steal, are greedy, get drunk, lie about others, or rob—these people will not inherit God's kingdom. In the past, some of you were like that, but you were washed clean. You were made holy, and you were made right with God in the name of the Lord Jesus Christ and in the Spirit of our God.

1 Corinthians 6:9-11

"I am allowed to do all things," but all things are not good for me to do. "I am allowed to do all things," but I will not let anything make me its slave. "Food is for the stomach, and the stomach for food," but God will destroy them both. The body is not for sexual sin but for the Lord, and the Lord is for the body.

1 Corinthians 6:12-13

So run away from sexual sin. Every other sin people do is outside their bodies, but those who sin sexually sin against their own bodies. You should know that your body is a temple for the Holy Spirit who is in you. You have received the Holy Spirit from God. So you do not belong to yourselves.

1 Corinthians 6:18-19

God, your love is so precious! You protect people in the shadow of your wings.

Psalm 36:7

Let us live in a right way, like people who belong to the day. We should not have wild parties or get drunk. There should be no sexual sins of any kind, no fighting or jealousy. But clothe yourself with the Lord Jesus Christ and forget about satisfying your sinful self.

Romans 13:13-14

Straight Talk From God's Word About Drugs and Alcohol

Do not be drunk with wine, which will ruin you, but be filled with the Spirit.

Ephesians 5:18

You should know that your body is a temple for the Holy Spirit who is in you. You have received the Holy Spirit from God. So you do not belong to yourselves, because you were bought by God for a price. So honor God with your bodies.

1 Corinthians 6:19-20

A thief comes to steal and kill and destroy, but I came to give life—life in all its fullness.

John 10:10

If we say we have no sin, we are fooling ourselves, and the truth is not in us. But if we confess our sins, he will forgive our sins, because we can trust God to do what is right. He will cleanse us from all the wrongs we have done.

1 John 1:8-9

The "night" is almost finished, and the "day" is almost here. So we should stop doing things that belong to darkness and take up the weapons used for fighting in the light. Let us live in a right way, like people who belong to the day. We should not have wild parties or get drunk. There should be no sexual sins of any kind, no fighting or jealousy. But clothe yourselves with the Lord Jesus Christ and forget about satisfying your sinful self.

Romans 13:12-14

Listen, my child, and be wise. Keep your mind on what is right. Don't drink too much wine or eat too much food. Those who drink and eat too much become poor. They sleep too much and end up wearing rags. Learn the truth and never reject it. Get wisdom, self-control, and understanding.

Proverbs 23:19-21, 23

Give all your worries to him, because he cares about you. Control yourselves and be careful! The devil, your enemy, goes around like a roaring lion looking for someone to eat.

1 Peter 5:7-8

Straight Talk From God's Word About Dating

You are not the same as those who do not believe. So do not join yourselves to them. Good and bad do not belong together. Light and darkness cannot share together. How can Christ and Belial, the devil, have any agreement? What can a believer have together with a nonbeliever? The temple of God cannot have any agreement with idols, and we are the temple of the living God. As God said: "I will live with them and walk with them. And I will be their God, and they will be my people."

2 Corinthians 6:14–16

So God created human beings in his image. In the image of God he created them. He created them male and female.

Genesis 1:27

Marriage should be honored by everyone, and husband and wife should keep their marriage pure. God will judge as guilty those who take part in sexual sins.

Hebrews 13:4

If you love me, you will obey my commands.

John 14:15

Jesus answered, "Love the Lord your God with all your heart, all your soul, and all your mind. This is the first and most important command. And the second command is like the first: Love your neighbor as you love yourself."

Matthew 22:37-39

Let us think about each other and help each other to show love and do good deeds.

Hebrews 10:24

Straight Talk From God's Word About Church

His goal was to carry out his plan, when the right time came, that all things in heaven and on earth would be joined together in Christ as the head. God put everything under his power and made him the head over everything for the church, which is Christ's body. The church is filled with Christ, and Christ fills everything in every way.

Ephesians 1:10, 22-23

God has freed us from the power of darkness, and he brought us into the kingdom of his dear Son. He is the head of the body, which is the church. Everything comes from him. He is the first one who was raised from the dead. So in all things Jesus has first place.

Colossians 1:13, 18

You should not stay away from the church meetings, as some are doing, but you should meet together and encourage each other.

Hebrews 10:25

No one ever hates his own body, but feeds and takes care of it. And that is what Christ does for the church, because we are parts of his body.

Ephesians 5:29–30

Be sure that no one leads you away with false and empty teaching that is only human, which comes from the ruling spirits of this world, and not from Christ. All of God lives in Christ fully (even when Christ was on earth), and you have a full and true life in Christ, who is ruler over all rulers and powers.

Colossians 2:8–10

Each one of us has a body with many parts, and these parts all have different uses. In the same way, we are many, but in Christ we are all one body. Each one is a part of that body, and each part belongs to all the other parts. We all have different gifts, each of which came because of the grace God gave us. The person who has the gift of prophecy should use that gift in agreement with the faith. Anyone who has the gift of serving should serve. Anyone who has the gift of teaching should teach. Whoever has the gift of encouraging others should encourage. Whoever has the gift of giving to others should give freely. Anyone who has the gift of being a leader should try hard when he leads. Whoever has the gift of showing mercy to others should do so with joy.

Romans 12:4-8

It is good and pleasant when God's people live together in peace!

Psalm 133:1

Straight Talk From God's Word About Following Christ

Then Barnabas went to the city of Tarsus to look for Saul, and when he found Saul, he brought him to Antioch. For a whole year Saul and Barnabas met with the church and taught many people there. In Antioch the followers were called Christians for the first time.

Acts 11:25-26

Jesus said to all of them, "If people want to follow me, they must give up the things they want. They must be willing to give up their lives daily to follow me. Those who want to save their lives will give up true life. But those who give their lives for me will have true life."

Luke 9:23-24

If anyone comes to me but loves his father, mother, wife, children, brothers, or sisters—or even life—more than me, he cannot be my follower.

Luke 14:26

As they were going along the road, someone said to Jesus, "I will follow you any place you go." Jesus said to them, "The foxes have holes to live in, and the birds have nests, but the Son of Man has no place to rest his head."

Luke 9:57-62

Whoever serves me must follow me.
Then my servant will be with me
everywhere I am. My Father will
honor anyone who serves me.

John 12:26

After this, Jesus went out and saw a tax collector named Levi sitting in the tax collector's booth. Jesus said to him, "Follow me!" So Levi got up, left everything, and followed him.

Luke 5:27-28

I think that all things are worth nothing compared with the greatness of knowing Christ Jesus my Lord. Because of him, I have lost all those things, and now I know they are worthless trash. This allows me to have Christ and to belong to him.

Philippians 3:8-9

You should teach people whom you can trust the things you and many others have heard me say. Then they will be able to teach others.

2 Timothy 2:2

Straight Talk From God's Word About Giving to God

Remember this: The person who plants a little will have a small harvest, but the person who plants a lot will have a big harvest. Each one should give as you have decided in your heart to give. You should not be sad when you give, and you should not give because you feel forced to forced to give. God loves the person who gives happily. And God can give you more blessings than you need. Then you will always have plenty of everything—enough to give to every good work.

2 Corinthians 9:6–8

In all the work you are doing, work the best you can. Work as if you were doing it for the Lord, not for people. Remember that you will receive your reward from the Lord, which he promised to his people. You are serving the Lord Christ.

Colossians 3:23–24

Each of you has received a gift to use to serve others. Be good servants of God's various gifts of grace. Anyone who speaks should speak words from God. Anyone who serves should serve with the strength God gives so that in everything God will be praised through Jesus Christ. Power and glory belong to him forever and ever. Amen.

1 Peter 4:10–11

Nothing in all the world can be hidden from God. Everything is clear and lies open before him, and to him we must explain the way we have lived.

Hebrews 4:13

Don't store treasures for yourselves here on earth where moths and rust will destroy them and thieves can break in and steal them. But store your treasures in heaven where they cannot be destroyed by moths or rust and where thieves cannot break in and steal them. Your heart will be where your treasure is.

Matthew 6:19–21

The thing you should want most is God's kingdom and doing what God wants. Then all these other things you need will be given to you.

Matthew 6:33

Some people give much but get back even more. Others don't give what they should and end up poor.

Whoever gives to others will get richer; those who help others will themselves be helped.

Proverbs 11:24-25

Whoever can be trusted with a little can also be trusted with a lot, and whoever is dishonest with a little is dishonest with a lot.

Luke 16:10

When we have the opportunity to help anyone, we should do it. But we should give special attention to those who are in the family of believers.

Galatians 6:10

Our only goal is to please God whether we live here or there, because we must all stand before Christ to be judged. Each of us will receive what we should get—good or bad—for the things we did in the earthly body.

2 Corinthians 5:9-10

Straight Talk From God's Word About Being Like Jesus

We must become like a mature person, growing until we become like Christ and have his perfection.

Ephesians 4:13

We must not become tired of doing good. We will receive our harvest of eternal life at the right time if we do not give up. When we have the opportunity to help anyone, we should do it. But we should give special attention to those who are in the family of believers.

Galatians 6:9-10

God has chosen you and made you his holy people. He loves you. So always do these things: Show mercy to others, be kind, humble, gentle, and patient. Get along with each other, and forgive each other. If someone does wrong to you, forgive that person because the Lord forgave you. Do all these things; but most important, love each other. Love is what holds you all together in perfect unity. Let the peace that Christ gives control your thinking, because you were all called together in one body to have peace. Always be thankful. Let the teaching of Christ live in you richly. Use all wisdom to teach and instruct each other by singing psalms, hymns, and spiritual songs with thankfulness in your hearts to God. Everything you do or say should be done to obey Jesus your Lord. And in all you do, give thanks to God the Father through Jesus.

Colossians 3:12-17

Lord, who may enter your Holy Tent? Who may live on your holy mountain? Only those who are innocent and who do what is right. Such people speak the truth from their hearts and do not tell lies about others. They do no wrong to their neighbors and do not gossip. They do not respect hateful people but honor those who honor the Lord. They keep their promises to their neighbors, even when it hurts. They do not charge interest on money they lend and do not take money to hurt innocent people. Whoever does all these things will never be destroyed.

Psalm 15:1-5

But the Spirit produces the fruit of love, joy, peace, patience, kindness, goodness, faithfulness, gentleness, self-control. There is no law that says these things are wrong. Those who belong to Christ Jesus have crucified their own sinful selves. They have given up their old selfish feelings and the evil things they wanted to do.

Ephesians 5:22-24

Straight Talk From God's Word About How to Be a Christian

Jesus said to his followers, "Go everywhere in the world, and tell the Good News to everyone."

Mark 16:15

You are the salt of the earth. But if the salt loses its salty taste, it cannot be made salty again. It is good for nothing, except to be thrown out and walked on. You are the light that gives light to the world. A city that is built on a hill cannot be hidden. And people don't hide a light under a bowl. They put it on a lampstand so the light shines for all the people in the house. In the same way, you should be a light for other people. Live so that they will see the good things you do and will praise your Father in heaven.

Matthew 5:13-16

"I was hungry, and you gave me food. I was thirsty, and you gave me something to drink. I was alone and away from home, and you invited me into your house. I was without clothes, and you gave me something to wear. I was sick, and you cared for me. I was in prison, and you visited me." Then the good people will answer, "Lord, when did we see you hungry and give you food, or thirsty and give you something to drink? When did we see you alone and away from home and invite you into our house? When did we see you without clothes and give you something to wear? When did we see you sick or in prison and care for you?" Then the King will answer, "I tell you the truth, anything you did for even the least of my people here, you also did for me."

Matthew 25:35-40

Those who give one of these little ones a cup of cold water because they are my followers will truly get their reward.

Matthew 10:42

Whoever does not care for his own relatives, especially his own family members, has turned against the faith and is worse than someone who does not believe in God.

1 Timothy 5:8

Brothers and sisters, if someone in your group does something wrong, you who are spiritual should go to that person and gently help make him right again. But be careful, because you might be tempted to sin, too. By helping each other with your troubles, you truly obey the law of Christ.

Galatians 6:14

My children, we should love people not only with words and talk, but by our actions and true caring. And God gives us what we ask for because we obey God's commands and do what pleases him. This is what God commands: that we believe in his Son, Jesus Christ, and that we love each other, just as he commanded.

1 John 3:18-23

What The
Bible Has To
Say About . . .

What The Bible Has
To Say About Faith

So faith comes from hearing the Good News, and people hear the Good News when someone tells them about Christ.

Romans 10:17

Because God has given me a special gift, I have something to say to everyone among you. Do not think you are better than you are. You must decide what you really are by the amount of faith God has given you.

Romans 12:3

We have around us many people whose lives tell us what faith means. So let us run the race that is before us and never give up. We should remove from our lives anything that would get in the way and the sin that so easily holds us back. Let us look only to Jesus, the One who began our faith and who makes it perfect.

Hebrews 12:1-2

Jesus answered, "Because your faith is too small. I tell you the truth, if your faith is as big a mustard seed, you can say to this mountain, 'Move from here to there,' and it will move. All things will be possible for you."

Matthew 17:20

Jesus said to the father, "You said, 'If you can!' All things are possible for the one who believes." Immediately the father cried out, "I do believe! Help me to believe more!"

Mark 9:23–24

We live by what we believe,
not by what we can see.

2 Corinthians 5:7

Without faith no one can please God. Anyone who comes to God must believe that he is real and that he rewards those who truly want to find him.

Hebrews 11:6

After Jesus went inside, the blind men went with him. He asked the men, "Do you believe that I can make you see again?" They answered, "Yes, Lord." Then Jesus touched their eyes and said, "Because you believe I can make you see again, it will happen."

Matthew 9:28–29

What The Bible Has To Say About Love

Dear friends, we should love each other, because love comes from God. Everyone who loves has become God's child and knows God. Whoever does not love does not know God, because God is love.

1 John 4:7-8

I may speak in different languages of people or even angels. But if I do not have love, I am only a noisy bell or a crashing cymbal. I may have the gift of prophecy. I may understand all the secret things of God and have all knowledge, and I may have faith so great I can move mountains. But even with all these things, if I do not have love, then I am nothing. I may give away everything I have, and I may even give my body as an offering to be burned. But I gain nothing if I do not have love. Love is patient and kind. Love is not jealous, it does not brag, and it is not proud. Love is not rude, is not selfish, and does not get upset with others. Love does not count up wrongs that have been done. Love is not happy with evil but is happy with the truth. Love patiently accepts all things. It always trusts, always hopes, and always remains strong. Love never ends. There are gifts of prophecy, but they will be ended. There are gifts of speaking in different languages, but those gifts will stop. There is the gift of knowledge, but it will come to an end. So these three things continue forever: faith, hope, and love. And the greatest of these is love.

1 Corinthians 13:1-8, 13

This is what real love is: It is not our love for God; it is God's love for us in sending his Son to be the way to take away our sins. Dear friends, if God loved is that much we also should love each other. No one has ever seen God, but if we love each other, God lives in us, and his love is made perfect in us.

1 John 4:10-12

Those who know my commands and obey them are the ones who love me, and my Father will love those who love me. I will love them and will show myself to them.

John 14:21

This is my command: Love each other as I have loved you. The greatest love a person can show is to die for his friends. You are my friends if you do what I command you. This is my command: Love each other.

John 15:12-14, 17

[Jesus said] "Love the Lord your God with all your heart, all your soul, all your mind, and all your strength." The second command is this: "Love your neighbor as you love yourself." There are no commands more important than these.

Mark 12:30-31

And so we know the love that God has for us, and we trust that love. God is love. Those who live in love live in God, and God lives in them. We love because God first loved us. If people say, "I love God," but hate their brothers or sisters, they are liars. Those who do not love their brothers and sisters, whom they have seen, cannot love God, whom they have never seen. And God gave us this command: Those who love God must also love their brothers and sisters.

1 John 4:16, 19-21

And from far away the Lord appeared to his people and said, "I love you people with a love that will last forever. That is why I have continued showing you kindness."

Jeremiah 31:3

But God shows his great love for us in this way: Christ died for us while we were still sinners.

Romans 5:8

God loved the world so much that he gave his one and only Son so that whoever believes in him may not be lost, but have eternal life.

John 3:16

But in all these things we have full victory through God who showed his love for us. Yes, I am sure that neither death, nor life, nor angels, nor ruling spirits, nothing now, nothing in the future, no powers, nothing above us, nothing below us, nor anything else in the whole world will ever be able to separate us from the love of God that is in Christ Jesus our Lord.

Romans 8:37–39

What The Bible Has To Say About Eternal Life

This is what God told us: God has given us eternal life, and this life is in his Son. Whoever has the Son has life, but whoever does not have the Son of God does not have life.

1 John 5:11-12

God loved the world so much that he gave his one and only Son so that whoever believes in him may not be lost, but have eternal life. God did not send his Son into the world to judge the world guilty, but to save the world through him.

John 3:16-17

Here is the bread that comes down from heaven. Anyone who eats this bread will never die. I am the living bread that came down from heaven. Anyone who eats this bread will live forever. This bread is my flesh, which I will give up so that the world may have life.

John 6:50-51

Jesus said to her, "I am the resurrection and the life. Those who believe in me will have life even if they die.

And everyone who lives and believes in me will never die."

John 11:25-26

My sheep listen to my voice; I know them, and they follow me. I give them eternal life, and they will never die, and no one can steal them out of my hand.

John 10:27-28

What The Bible Has To Say About Death

See, even wise people die. Fools and stupid people also die and leave their wealth to others. Even rich people do not live forever; like the animals, people die. But God will save my life and will take me from the grave.

Psalm 49:10, 12, 15

I tell you the truth, whoever obeys my teaching will never die.

John 8:51

It is now shown to us by the coming of our Savior Christ Jesus. He destroyed death, and through the Good News he showed us the way to have life that cannot be destroyed.

2 Timothy 1:10

Respect for the Lord gives life. It is like a fountain that can save people from death. The wicked are ruined by their own evil, but those who do right are protected even in death.

Proverbs 14:27, 32

If we live, we are living for the Lord, and if we die,

we are dying for the Lord. So living or dying, we belong to the Lord. The reason Christ died and rose from the dead to live again was so he would be Lord over both the dead and the living.

Romans 14:8-9

Just as the Father raises the dead and gives them life, so also the Son gives life to those he wants to. I tell you the truth, whoever hears what I say and believes in the One who sent me has eternal life. That person will not be judged guilty but has already left death and entered life.

John 5:21, 24

What The Bible Has To Say About Praising God

The people I made will sing songs to praise me.

Isaiah 43:21

But you are a chosen people, royal priests, a holy nation, a people for God's own possession. You were chosen to tell about the wonderful acts of God, who called you out of darkness into his wonderful light.

1 Peter 2:9

Here on earth we do not have a city that lasts forever, but we are looking for the city that we will have in the future. So through Jesus let us always offer to God our sacrifice of praise, coming from lips that speak his name.

Hebrews 13:14–15

Praise the Lord! It is good to sing praises to our God; it is good and pleasant to praise him.

Psalm 147:1

I will call to the Lord, who is worthy of praise, and I will be saved from my enemies.

2 Samuel 22:4

I will praise the Lord at all times; his praise is always on my lips. My whole being praises the Lord. The poor will hear and be glad. Glorify theLord with me, and let us praise his name together.

Psalm 34:1-3

Let them give thanks to the Lord for his love and for the miracles he does for people.

Psalm 107:8

Clap your hands, all you people. Shout to God with joy. The Lord Most High is wonderful He is the great King over all the earth! Sing praises to God. Sing praises. Sing praises to our King. Sing praises. God is King of all the earth, so sing a song of praise to him.

Psalm 47:1-2, 6-7

The Lord is great; he should be praised in the city of our God, on his holy mountain.

Psalm 48:1

Those people honor me who bring me offerings to show thanks. And I, God, will save those who do that.

Psalm 50:23

Because your love is better than life, I will praise

you. I will praise you as long as I live. I will lift up my hands in prayer to your name. I will be content as if I had eaten the best foods. My lips will sing, and my mouth will praise you.

Psalm 63:3-5

Lord, you are my hope. Lord, I have trusted you since I was young. I have depended on you since I was born; you helped me even on the day of my birth. I will always praise you. I am an example to many people, because you are my strong protection. I am always praising you; all day long I honor you.

Psalm 71:5-8

It is good to praise to God Most High. It is good to tell of your love in the morning and of your loyalty at night. Lord, you have made me happy by what you have done; I will sing for joy about what your hands have done. Lord, you have done such great things! How deep are your thoughts!

Psalm 92:1-2, 4-5

About midnight Paul and Silas were praying and singing songs to God as the other prisoners listened.

Acts 16:25

What The Bible Has To Say About Serving God

Serve only the Lord your God. Respect him, keep his commands, and obey him. Serve him and be loyal to him.

Deuteronomy 13:4

No one can serve two masters. The person will hate one master and love the other, or will follow one master and refuse to follow the other. You cannot serve both God and worldly riches.

Matthew 6:24

Jesus said to the devil, "Go away from me, Satan! It is written in the Scriptures, 'You must worship the Lord your God and serve only him.'" So the devil left Jesus, and angels came and took care of him.

Matthew 4:10-11

Shout to the Lord, all the earth. Serve the Lord with joy; come before him with singing.

Psalm 100:1-2

Now, Israel, this is what the Lord your God wants you to do: Respect the Lord your God, and do what he has told you to do. Love him. Serve the Lord your God with your whole being, and obey the Lord's commands and laws that I am giving you today for your own good.

Deuteronomy 10:12-13

But if you don't want to serve the Lord, you must choose for yourselves today whom you will serve. . . . As for me and my family, we will serve the Lord.

Joshua 24:15

Young people, enjoy yourselves while you are young; be happy while you are young. Do whatever your heart desires, whatever you want to do. But remember that God will judge you for everything you do.

Ecclesiastes 11:9

What The Bible Has To Say About God's Grace

You gave me life and showed me kindness, and in your care you watched over my life.

Job 10:12

Because of his love, God had already decided to make us his own children through Jesus Christ. That was what he wanted and what pleased him, and it brings praise to God because of his wonderful grace. God gave that grace to us freely, in Christ, the One he loves. In Christ we are set free by the blood of his death, and so we have forgiveness of sins. How rich is God's grace.

Ephesians 1:5–7

Those who find me find life, and the Lord will be pleased with them.

Proverbs 8:35

But God's grace has made me what I am, and his grace to me was not wasted.

1 Corinthians 15:10

But God's mercy is great, and he loved us very much. Though we were spiritually dead because of the things we did against God, he gave us new life with Christ. You have been saved by God's grace. And he raised us up with Christ and gave us a seat with him in the heavens. He did this for those in Christ Jesus so that for all future time he could show the very great riches of his grace by being kind to us in Christ Jesus. I mean that you have been saved by grace through believing. You did not save yourselves; it was a gift from God.

Ephesians 2:4–8

All these things are for you. And so the grace of God that is being given to more and more and more people will bring increasing thanks to God for his glory.

2 Corinthians 4:15

Let us, then, feel very sure that we can come before God's throne where there is grace. There we can receive mercy and grace to help us when we need it.

Hebrews 4:16

What The Bible Has To Say About the Holy Spirit

And this hope will never disappoint us, because God has poured out his love to fill our hearts. He gave us his love through the Holy Spirit, whom God has given to us.

Romans 5:5

[Jesus said] I will ask the Father, and he will give you another Helper to be with you forever—the Spirit of truth. The world cannot accept him, because it does not see him or know him. But you know him, because he lives with you and he will be in you.

John 14:16-17

[Jesus said] But I tell you the truth, it is better for you that I go away. When I go away, I will send the Helper to you. If I do not go away, the Helper will not come. When the Helper comes, he will prove to the people of the world the truth about sin, about being right with God, and about judgment. He will prove to them that sin is not believing in me. The Spirit of truth will bring glory to me, because he will take what I have to say and tell it to you.

John 16:7-9, 14

Once when he was eating with them, he told them not to leave Jerusalem. He said, "Wait here to receive the promise from the Father which I told you about. John baptized people with water, but in a few days you will be baptized with the Holy Spirit." Jesus said to them, "The Father is the only One who has the authority to decide dates and times. These things are not for you to know. But when the Holy Spirit comes to you, you will receive power. You will be my witnesses—in Jerusalem, in all of Judea, in Samaria, and in every part of the world."

Acts 1:4-5, 7-8

Peter said to them, "Change your hearts and lives and be baptized, each one of you, in the name of Jesus Christ for the forgiveness of your sins. And you will receive the gift of the Holy Spirit."

Acts 2:38

After they had prayed, the place where they were meeting was shaken. They were all filled with the Holy Spirit, and they spoke God's word without fear.

Acts 4:31

While Peter was still saying this, the Holy Spirit came down on all those who were listening. The Jewish believers who came with Peter were amazed that the gift of the Holy Spirit had been given even to those who were not Jews. These Jewish believers heard them speaking in different languages and praising God. Then Peter said, "Can anyone keep these people from being baptized with water? They have received the Holy Spirit just as we did!"

Acts 10:44-47

What The Bible Has To Say About God's Faithfulness

Lord, your love fills the earth. Teach me your demands. You have done good things for your servant, as you have promised, Lord.

Psalm 119:64-65

The Lord says, "This day is like the time of Noah to me. I promised then that I would never flood the world again. In the same way, I promise I will not be angry with you or punish you again. The mountains may disappear, and the hills may come to an end, but my love will never disappear; my promise of peace will not come to an end," says the Lord who shows mercy to you.

Isaiah 54:9-10

"When the rainbow appears in the clouds, I will see it and I will remember the agreement that continues forever between me and every living thing on the earth." So God said to Noah, "The rainbow is a sign of the agreement that I made with all living things on earth."

Genesis 9:16-17

God, who has called you to share everything with his Son, Jesus Christ our Lord, is faithful.

1 Corinthians 1:9

If we are not faithful, he will still be faithful, because he cannot be false to himself.

2 Timothy 2:13

But the Lord chose you because he loved you, and he kept his promise to your ancestors. So he brought you out of Egypt by his great power and freed you from the land of slavery, from the power of the king of Egypt. So know that the Lord your God is God, the faithful God. He will keep his agreement of love for a thousand lifetimes for people who love him and obey his commands.

Deuteronomy 7:8–9

Lord, your love reaches to the heavens, your loyalty to the skies.

Psalm 36:5

I will always sing about the Lord's love; I will tell of his loyalty from now on. I will say, "Your love continues forever; your loyalty goes on and on like the sky."

Psalm 89:1–2

What The Bible Has To Say About Satan

Control yourselves and be careful! The devil, your enemy, goes around like a roaring lion looking for someone to eat. Refuse to give in to him, by standing strong in your faith.

1 Peter 5:8-9

So give yourselves completely to God. Stand against the devil, and the devil will run from you. Come near to God, and God will come near to you. You sinners, clean sin out of your lives. You who are trying to follow God and the world at the same time, make your thinking pure.

James 4:7-8

God has freed us from the power of darkness, and he brought us into the kingdom of his dear Son.

Colossians 1:13

The God who brings peace will soon defeat Satan and give you power over him. The grace of our Lord Jesus be with you.

Romans 16:20

Then I heard a loud voice in heaven saying: "The salvation and the power and the kingdom of our God and the authority of his Christ have now come. The accuser of our brothers and sisters, who accused them day and night before our God, has been thrown down. And our brothers and sisters defeated him by the blood of the Lamb's death and by the message they preached. They did not love their lives so much that they were afraid of death."

Revelation 12:10-11

We do live in the world, but we do not fight in the same way the world fights. We fight with weapons that are different from those the world uses. Our weapons have power from God that can destroy the enemy's strong places. We destroy people's arguments and every proud thing that raises itself against the knowledge of God. We capture every thought and make it give up and obey Christ.

2 Corinthians 10:3-5

Dear children, do not let anyone lead you the wrong way. Christ is all that is right. So to be like Christ a person must do what is right. The devil has been sinning since the beginning, so anyone who continues to sin belongs to the devil. The Son of God came for this purpose: to destroy the devil's work.

1 John 3:7-8

What The Bible Has To Say About Spiritual Battles

Finally, be strong in the Lord and in his great power. Put on the full armor of God so that you can fight against the devil's evil tricks. Our fight is not against people on earth but against the rulers and authorities and the powers of this world's darkness, against the spiritual powers of evil in the heavenly world. . . . . So stand strong, with the belt of truth tied around your waist and the protection of right living on your chest. On your feet wear the Good News of peace to help you stand strong. And also use the shield of faith with which you can stop all the burning arrows of the Evil One. Accept God's salvation as your helmet, and take the sword of the Spirit, which is the word of God. Pray in the Spirit at all times with all kinds of prayers, asking for everything you need. To do this you must always be ready and never give up. Always pray for all God's people.

Ephesians 6:10–18

Don't let anyone use magic or witchcraft, or try to explain the meaning of signs. Don't let anyone try to control others with magic, and don't let them be mediums or try to talk with the spirits of dead people. The Lord hates anyone who does these things. Because the other nations do these things, the Lord your God will force them out of the land ahead of you. But you must be innocent I the presence of the Lord your God. The nations you will force out listen to people who use magic and witchcraft, but the Lord your God will not let you do those things.

Deuteronomy 18:10-14

We do live in the world, but we do not fight in the same way the world fights. We fight with weapons that are different from those the world uses. Our weapons have power from God that can destroy the enemy's strong places. We destroy people's arguments and every proud thing that raises itself against the knowledge of God. We capture every thought and make it give up and obey Christ.

2 Corinthians 10:3-5

What The Bible Has To Say About Hell

But cowards, those who refuse to believe, who do evil things, who kill, who sin sexually, who do evil magic, who worship idols, and who tell lies—all these will have a place in the lake of burning sulfur. This is the second death.

Revelation 21:8

Don't be afraid of people, who can kill the body but cannot kill the soul. The only one you should fear is the one who can destroy the soul and the body in hell.

Matthew 10:28

And the tongue is like a fire. It is a whole world of evil among the parts of our bodies. The tongue spreads its evil through the whole body. The tongue is set on fire by hell, and it starts a fire that influences all of life.

James 3:6

And he will give rest to you who are troubled and to us also when the Lord Jesus appears with burning fire from heaven with his powerful angels. Then he will punish those who do not know God and who do not obey the Good News abut our Lord Jesus Christ.

Those people will be punished with a destruction that continues forever. They will be kept away from the Lord and his great power.

2 Thessalonians 1:7-9

These people will go off to be punished forever, but the good people will go to live forever.

Matthew 25:46

The Son of Man will send out his angels, and they will gather out of his kingdom all who cause sin and all who do evil. The angels will throw them into the blazing furnace, where the people will cry and grind their teeth with pain.

Matthew 13:41-42

When angels sinned, God did not let them go free without punishment. He sent them to hell and put them in caves of darkness where they are being held for judgment.

2 Peter 2:4

In hell the worm does not die; the fire is never put out. Every person will be salted with fire.

Mark 9:48-49

What The Bible Has To Say About The Return of Christ

They said, "Men of Galilee, why are you standing here looking into the sky? Jesus, whom you saw taken up from you into heaven, will come back in the same way you saw him go."

Acts 1:11

That is the way we should live, because God's grace that can save everyone has come. It teaches us not to live against God nor to do the evil things the world wants to do. Instead, that grace teaches us to live now in a wise and right way and in a way that shows we serve God. We should live like that while we wait for our great hope and the coming of the glory of our great God and Savior Jesus Christ.

Titus 2:11-13

When the Son of Man comes, he will be seen by everyone, like lightening flashing from the east to the west. Soon after the trouble of those days, the sun will grow dark, and the moon will not give light. The stars will fall from the sky. And the powers of the heavens will be shaken. At that time, the sign of the Son of Man will appear in the sky. Then all the peoples of the world will cry. They will see the Son of Man coming on clouds in the sky with great power and glory. He will use a loud trumpet to send his angels all around the earth, and they will gather his chosen people from every part of the world.

Matthew 24:27, 29-31

Dear friends, now we are children of God, and we have not yet been shown what we will be in the future. But we know that when Christ comes again, we will be like him, because we will see him as he really is. Christ is pure, and all who have this hope in Christ keep themselves pure like Christ.

1 John 3:2-3

Now the Holy Spirit clearly says that in the later times some people will stop believing the faith. They will follow spirits that lie and teachings of demons.

1 Timothy 4:1

No one knows when that day or time will be, not the angels in heaven, not even the Son. Only the Father knows.

Matthew 24:36

Jesus said, "Don't let your hearts be troubled. Trust in God, and trust in me. There are many rooms in my Father's house; I would not tell you this if it were not true. I am going there to prepare a place for you. After I go and prepare a place for you, I will come back and take you to be with me so that you may be where I am. You know the way to the place where I am going."

John 14:1-4

Truth From
The Bible
About . . .

Truth From The Bible About God's Will for Your Life

But if any of you needs wisdom, you should ask God for it. He is generous and enjoys giving to all people, so he will give you wisdom. But when you ask God, you must believe and not doubt. Anyone who doubts is like a wave in the sea, blown up and down by the wind.

James 1:5-6

The Lord says, "I will make you wise and show you where to go. I will guide you and watch over you."

Psalm 32:8

Your word is like a lamp for my feet and a light for my path. I will do what I have promised and obey your fair laws.

Psalm 119:105-106

My son, keep your father's commands, and don't forget your mother's teaching. They will guide you when you walk. They will guard you when you sleep. They will speak to you when you are awake. These commands are like a lamp; this teaching is like a light. And the correction that comes from them will help you have life.

Proverbs 6:20, 22–23

Always remember what is written in the Book of the Teachings. Study it day and night to be sure to obey everything that is written there. If you do this, you will be wise and successful in everything.

Joshua 1:8

If you go the wrong way—to the right or to the left—you will hear a voice behind you saying, "This is the right way. You should go this way."

Isaiah 30:21

This God is our God forever and ever. He will guide us from now on.

Psalm 48:14

Teach me to do what you want, because you are my God. Let your good Spirit lead me on level ground.

Psalm 143:10

Depend on the Lord in whatever you do, and your plans will succeed.

Proverbs 16:3

When a person's steps follow the Lord, God is pleased with his ways. If he stumbles, he will not fall, because the Lord holds his hand.

Psalm 37:23–24

My child, do not forget my teaching, but keep my commands in mind. Trust the Lord with all your heart, and don't depend on your own understanding. Remember the Lord in all you do, and he will give you success. My child, do not reject the Lord's discipline, and don't get angry when he corrects you. The Lord corrects those he loves, just as parents correct the child they delight in.

Proverbs 3:1, 5–6, 11–12

This is what the Lord, who saves you, the Holy One of Israel, says: "I am the Lord your God, who teaches you to do what is good, who leads you in the way you should go."

Isaiah 48:17

The Lord will always lead you. He will satisfy your needs in dry lands and give strength to your bones. You will be like a garden that has much water, like a spring that never runs dry.

Isaiah 58:11

Do not change yourselves to be like the people of this world, but be changed within by a new way of thinking. Then you will be able to decide what God wants for you; you will know what is good and pleasing to him and what is perfect.

Romans 12:2

You are my rock and my protection.
For the good of your name, lead me
and guide me. I give you my life.
Save me, Lord, God of truth.

Psalm 31:3, 5

The true children of God are those who let God's Spirit lead them.

Romans 8:14

So do not be foolish but learn what the Lord wants you to do.

Ephesians 5:17

Truth From The
Bible About Prayer

I will provide for their needs before they ask, and I will help them while they are still asking for help.

Isaiah 65:24

Ask, and God will give to you. Search, and you will find. Knock, and the door will open for you. Yes, everyone who asks will receive. Everyone who searches will find. And everyone who knocks will have the door opened.

Matthew 7:7-8

Also, I tell you that if two of you on earth agree about something and pray for it, it will be done for you by my Father in heaven. This is true because if two or three people come together in my name, I am there with them.

Matthew 18:19-20

So I tell you to believe that you have received the things you ask for in prayer, and God will give them to you. When you are praying, if you are angry with someone, forgive him so that your Father in heaven will also forgive your sins.

Mark 11:24-25

When you pray, you should go into your room and close the door and pray to your Father who cannot be seen. Your Father will give you anything you ask for in my name.

John 16:23

Let us, then, feel very sure that we can come before God's throne where there is grace. There we can receive mercy and grace to help us when we need it.

Hebrews 4:16

They will call to me, and I will answer them. I will be with them in trouble; I will rescue them and honor them. I will give them a long, full life, and they will see how I can save.

Psalm 91:15–16

The Lord is close to everyone who prays to him, to all who truly pray to him. He gives those who respect him what they want. He listens when they cry, and he saves them. The Lord protects everyone who loves him, but he will destroy the wicked.

Psalm 145:18–20

The Lord does not listen to the wicked, but he hears the prayers of those who do right.

Proverbs 15:29

Truth From The Bible About People Who Are Not Saved

All have sinned and are not good enough for God's glory, and all need to be made right with God by his grace, which is a free gift. They need to be made free from sin through Jesus Christ.

Romans 3:23–24

God's anger is shown from heaven against all the evil and wrong things people do. By their own evil lives they hide the truth. God shows his anger because some knowledge of him has been made clear to them. Yes, God has shown himself to them. There are things about him that people cannot see—his eternal power and all the things that make him God. But since the beginning of the world those things have been easy to understand by what God has made. So people have no excuse for the bad things they do.

Romans 1:18–20

But God shows his great love for us in this way: Christ died for us while we were still sinners. So through Christ we will surely be saved from God's anger, because we have been made right with God by the blood of Christ's death.

Romans 5:8–9

[Jesus said] I have not come to invite good people but sinners to change their hearts and lives.

Luke 5:32

The Son of man came to find lost people and save them.

Luke 19:10

Jesus answered, "I tell you the truth, unless one is born again, he cannot be in God's kingdom."

John 3:3

By the words he will say to you, you and all your family will be saved.

Acts 1 1:14

If a man has a hundred sheep but one of the sheep gets lost, he will leave the other ninety-nine on the hill and go to look for the lost sheep. In the same way, your Father in heaven does not want any of these little children to be lost.

Matthew 18:12, 14

Truth From The Bible About Your Family

When you talk, do not say harmful things, but say what people need—words that will help others become stronger. Then what you say will do good to those who listen to you. And do not make the Holy Spirit sad. The Spirit is God's proof that you belong to him. God gave you the Spirit to show that God will make you free when the final day comes. Do not be bitter or angry or mad. Never shout angrily or say things to hurt others. Never do anything evil. Be kind and loving to each other, and forgive each other just as God forgave you in Christ.

Ephesians 4:29-32

They said to him, "Believe in the Lord Jesus and you will be saved—you and all the people in your house."

Acts 16:31

Honor your father and your mother so that you will live a long time in the land that the Lord your God is going to give you.

Exodus 20:12

Old people are proud of their grandchildren, and children are proud of their parents. A friend loves you all the time, and a brother helps in time of trouble. A foolish son makes his father sad and causes his mother great sorrow.

Proverbs 17:6, 17, 25

The father of a good child is very happy; parents who have wise children are glad because of them. Make your father and mother happy; give your mother a reason to be glad.

Proverbs 23:24-25

My child, listen and accept what I say. Then you will have a long life. I am guiding you in the way of wisdom, and I am leading you on the right path.

Proverbs 4:10-11

God has chosen you and made you his holy people. He loves you. So always do these things: Show mercy to others, be kind, humble, gentle, and patient. Get along with each other, and forgive each other. If someone does wrong to you, forgive that person because the Lord forgave you.

Colossians 3:12-12

I give you a new command: Love each other. You must love each other as I have loved you. All people will know that you are my followers if you love each other.

John 13:34-35

Always be humble, gentle, and patient, accepting each other in love. You are joined together with peace through the Spirit, so make every effort to continue together in this way.

Ephesians 4:2-3

Do everything without complaining or arguing. Then you will be innocent and without any wrong. You will be God's children without any fault. But you are living with crooked and mean people all around you, among who you shine like stars in the dark world.

Philippians 2:14-15

Love each other like brothers and sisters. Give each other more honor than you want for yourselves.

Romans 12:10

What You Can Do To . . .

What You Can Do To Make Every Day Count for God

Teach us how short our lives really are so that we may be wise.

Psalm 90:12

Do people really gain anything from their work? I saw the hard work God has given people to do. God has given them a desire to know the future. He does everything just right and on time, but people can never completely understand what he is doing. So I realize that the best thing for them is to be happy and enjoy themselves as long as they live. God wants all people to eat and drink and be happy in their work, which are gifts from God. I know that everything God does will continue forever. People cannot add anything to what God has done, and they cannot take anything away from it. God does it this way to make people respect him.

Ecclesiastes 3:9–14

Whoever obeys the king's command will be safe. A wise person does the right thing at the right time. There is a right time and a right way for everything, yet people often have many troubles. They do not know what the future holds, and no one can tell them what will happen.

Ecclesiastes 8:5-7

Don't wear yourself out trying to get rich; be wise enough to control yourself. Wealth can vanish in the wink of an eye. It can seem to grow wings and fly away like an eagle.

Proverbs 23:4-5

Spend time with the wise and you will become wise, but friends of fools will suffer.

Proverbs 13:20

A lazy person will end up poor, but a hard worker will become rich. Those who gather crops on time are wise, but those who sleep through the harvest are a disgrace.

Proverbs 10:4-5

It someone is lazy, the roof will begin to fall. If he doesn't fix it, the house will leak.

Ecclesiastes 10:18

The right word spoken at the right time is as beautiful as gold apples in a silver bowl.

Proverbs 25:11

The Lord sees everything you do, and he watches where you go.

Proverbs 5:21

What You Can Do
To Please God

Bring to me all the people who are mine, whom I made for my glory, whom I formed and made. The people I made will sing songs to praise me.

Isaiah 43:7, 21

The time is coming when the true worshipers will worship the Father in spirit and truth, and that time is here already. You see, the Father too is actively seeking such people to worship him. God is spirit, and those who worship him must worship in spirit and truth.

John 4:23-24

Those who blew the trumpets and those who sang together sounded like one person as they praised and thanked the Lord. They sang as others played their trumpets, cymbals, and other instruments. They praised the Lord with this song: "He is good; his love continues forever." Then the Temple of the Lord was filled with a cloud. The priests could not continue their work because of the cloud, because the Lord's glory filled the Temple of God.

2 Chronicles 5:13-14

You also are like living stones, so let yourselves be used to build a spiritual temple to be holy priests who offer spiritual sacrifices to God. He will accept those sacrifices through Jesus Christ. But you are a chosen people, royal priests, a holy nation, a people for God's own possession. You were chosen to tell about the wonderful acts of God, who called you out of darkness into his wonderful light.

1 Peter 2:5, 9

So through Jesus let us always offer to God our sacrifice of praise, coming from lips that speak his name. Do not forget to do good to others, and share with them, because such sacrifices please God.

Hebrews 13:15-16

You are worthy, our Lord and God, to receive glory and honor and power, because you made all things. Everything existed and was made, because you wanted it.

Revelation 4:11

Without faith no one can please God. Anyone who comes to God must believe that he is real and that he rewards those who truly want to find him.

Hebrews 11:6

I will thank the Lord very much; I will praise him in front of many people.

Psalm 109:30

And God gives us what we ask for because we obey God's commands and do what pleases him.

1 John 3:22

It is not fancy hair, gold jewelry, or fine clothes that should make you beautiful. No, your beauty should come from within you—the beauty of a gentle and quiet spirit that will never be destroyed and is very precious to God.

1 Peter 3:3-4

Since we know what it means to fear the Lord, we try to help people accept the truth about us. God knows what we really are, and I hope that in your hearts you know, too. We are not trying to prove ourselves to you again, but we are telling you about ourselves so you will be proud of us. Then you will have an answer for those who are proud about things that can be seen rather than what is in the heart.

2 Corinthians 5:11-12

What You Can Do
To Grow in Your Faith

But grow in the grace and knowledge of our Lord and Savior Jesus Christ. Glory be to him now and forever! Amen.

2 Peter 3:18

As newborn babies want milk, you should want the pure and simple teaching. By it you can grow up and be saved, because you have already examined and seen how good the Lord is.

1 Peter 2:2-3

Make every effort to give yourself to God as the kind of person he will accept. Be a worker who is not ashamed and who uses the true teaching in the right way.

2 Timothy 2:15

Continue to do those things; give your life to doing them so your progress may be seen by everyone.

1 Timothy 4:15

So let us go on to grown-up teaching. Let us not go back over the beginning lessons we learned about

Christ. We should not again start teaching about faith in God and about turning away from those acts that lead to death.

Hebrews 6:1

Because you have these blessings, do your best to add these things to your lives: to your faith, add goodness; and to your goodness, add knowledge; and to your knowledge, add self-control; and to your self-control, add patience; and to your patience, add service for God; and to your service for God, add kindness for your brothers and sisters in Christ; and to this kindness, add love. If all these things are in you and are growing, they will help you to be useful and productive in your knowledge of our Lord Jesus Christ.

2 Peter 1:5-8

Let the teaching of Christ live in you richly. Use all wisdom to teach and instruct each other by singing psalms, hymns, and spiritual songs with thankfulness in your hearts to God.

Colossians 3:16

God began doing a good work in you, and I am sure he will continue it until it is finished when Jesus Christ comes again. This is my prayer for you: that your love will grow more and more; that you will have knowledge and understanding with your love; that you will see the difference between good and bad and will choose the good; that you will be pure and without wrong for the coming of Christ.

Philippians 1:6, 9–10

Then we will no longer be babies. We will not be tossed about like a ship that the waves carry one way and then another. We will not be influenced by every new teaching we hear from people who are trying to fool us.

Ephesians 4:14

What You Can Do To Influence Your World

You are the light that gives light to the world. A city that is built on a hill cannot be hidden. And people don't hide a light under a bowl. They put it on a lampstand so the light shines for all the people in the house. In the same way, you should be a light for other people. Live so that they will see the good things you do and will praise your Father in heaven.

Matthew 5:14-16

The wise people will shine like the brightness of the sky. Those who teach others to live right will shine like stars forever and ever.

Daniel 12:3

Jesus said to his followers, "Go everywhere in the world and tell the Good News to every one. Anyone who believes and is baptized will be saved, but anyone who does not believe will be punished. And those who believe will be able to do these things as proof: They will use my name to force out demons. They will speak in new languages. They will pick up snakes and drink poison without being hurt. They will touch the sick, and the sick will be healed." After the Lord Jesus said these things to his followers, he was carried up into heaven, and he sat at the right side of God. The followers went everywhere in the world and told the Good News to people, and the Lord helped them. The Lord proved that the Good News they told was true by giving them power to work miracles.

Mark 16:15–20

I tell you the truth, whoever believes in me will do the same things that I do. Those who believe will do even greater things than these, because I am going to the Father.

John 14:12

I give you a new command: Love each other. You must love each other as I have loved you. All people will know that you are my followers if you love each other.

John 13:34–35

Loving God means obeying his commands. And God's commands are not too hard for us, because everyone who is a child of God conquers the world. And this is the victory that conquers the world—our faith. So the one who wins against the world is the person who believes that Jesus is the Son of God.

1 John 5:3–5

Do not change yourselves to be like the people of this world, but be changed within by a new way of thinking. Then you will be able to decide what God wants for you; you will know what is good and pleasing to him and what is perfect.

Romans 12:2

In the past, people did not understand God, and he ignored this. But now, God tells all people in the world to change their hearts and lives.

Acts 17:30

But before people can ask the Lord for help, they must believe in him; and before they can believe in him, they must hear about him; and for them to hear about the Lord, someone must tell them.

Romans 10:14

Jesus answered, "Everyone who drinks this water will be thirsty again, but whoever drinks the water I give will never be thirsty. The water I give will become a spring of water gushing up inside that person, giving eternal life."

John 4:13–14

God's Plan
of Salvation

God's Plan
of Salvation

Sin came into the world because of what one man did, and with sin came death. This is why everyone must die—because everyone sinned.

Romans 5:12

All have sinned and are not good enough for God's glory, and all need to be made right with God by his grace, which is a free gift. They need to be made free from sin through Jesus Christ.

Romans 3:23-24

When people sin, they earn what sin pays—death. But God gives us a free gift—life forever in Christ Jesus our Lord.

Romans 6:23

But God shows his great love for us in this way: Christ died for us while we were still sinners.

Romans 5:8

God did not send his Son into the world to judge the world guilty, but to save the world through him.

John 3:17

Those who believe in the Son have eternal life, but those who do not obey the Son will never have life. God's anger stays on them.

John 3:36

God loved the world so much that he gave his one and only Son so that whoever believes in him may not be lost, but have eternal life.

John 1:12

I mean that you have been saved by grace through believing. You did not save yourselves; it was a gift from God. It was not the result of your own efforts, so you cannot brag about it.

Ephesians 2:8–9

This is what the Scripture says: "The word is near you; it is in your mouth and in your heart." That is the teaching of faith that we are telling. If you use your mouth to say, "Jesus is Lord," and if you believe in your heart that God raised Jesus from the dead, you will be saved. We believe with our hearts, and so we are made right with God. And we use our mouths to say that we believe, and so we are saved.

Romans 10:8–10

All those who stand before others and say they believe in me, I will say before my Father in heaven that they belong to me.

Matthew 10:32

This is what God told us: God has given us eternal life, and this life is in his Son. Whoever has the Son has life, but whoever does not have the Son of God does not have life. I write this letter to you who believe in the Son of God so you will know you have eternal life.

1 John 5:11-13

Check out these other
Extreme for Jesus™ products:

Bibles

Extreme Teen Bible - Hard Cover
    0-7852-0081-9   *$24.99*

Extreme Teen Bible - Paperback
    0-7852-0082-7   *$19.99*

Extreme Teen Bible - Black Bonded Leather
    0-7852-5555-9   *$39.99*

Extreme Teen Bible - Deep Purple Bonded Leather
    0-7852-5525-7   *$39.99*

Extreme Teen Bible - Slimey Limey Green Bonded
    0-7852-5646-6   *$39.99*

Extreme Teen Bible - Lava Orange Bonded
    0-7852-5678-4   *$39.99*

Extreme Word GenX Bible - FlushCut
    0-7852-5732-2   *$19.99*

Extreme Word GenX Bible - Chromium Hard Cover
    0-7852-5733-0   *$29.99*

Extreme Word GenX Bible - Blue Snake Hard Cover
    0-7852-5796-9   *$29.99*

Extreme Word GenX Bible - Black Vinyl
    0-7852-5735-7   *$39.99*

Extreme Teen Bible (New Century Version) - Paperback
    0-7852-5834-5   *$19.99*

Extreme Teen Bible (New Century Version) - Hard Cover
0-7852-5835-3 $24.99
Gospel of John
0-7852-5537-0 $1.50

Books

Extreme A-Z: Find it in the Bible
0-7852-4580-4 $19.99
Extreme Answers to Extreme Questions
0-7852-4594-4 $12.99
Dictionary
0-7852-4611-8 $19.99
Extreme Journey
0-7852-4595-2 $14.99
Burn: A Call to Extreme Compassion
0-7852-6746-8 $9.99
Genuine (by Stacie Orrico - with CD single)
0-8499-9545-0 $13.99
Extreme Faith
0-7852-6757-3 $10.99

Devotionals

Extreme Encounters
0-7852-5657-1 $9.99

Journals

Xt4J Journal (Plastic Cover)
0-8499-5710-9   *$9.99*
Xt4J Journal (Leather Sky)
0-8499-9508-6   *$9.99*

Workbooks

Step Off
0-7852-4604-5   *$19.99*

Promise Books

Extreme for Jesus Promise Book (by Ron Luce)
0-8499-5606-4   *$13.99*

Calendars

No Repeat Days   *0-8499-9510-8*   *$9.99*

```
Be Extreme for Jesus
in your life . . .
Check it out! Get involved!
Make a difference!
```

Compassion International
God can use you to change the life of a child forever.
www.ci.org

Habitat for Humanity International
A Christian organization that welcomes volunteers
from all faiths who are committed to Habitat's goal
of eliminating poverty housing.
www.habitat.org

World Vision
For kids in need around the world, hope changes
everything.
www.worldvision.org

National Center for Family Literacy
Promoting family literacy across the United States.
www.famlit.org

Big Brothers Big Sisters of America
Making a big difference. One child at a time.
www.bbbsa.org

Americares
Bringing help and hope
www.americares.org

Volunteermatch.org
Thousands of volunteer opportunities on-line
www.volunteermatch.org

Notes

Notes

Notes

Notes

Notes

Notes

Notes

Notes

Notes

Notes

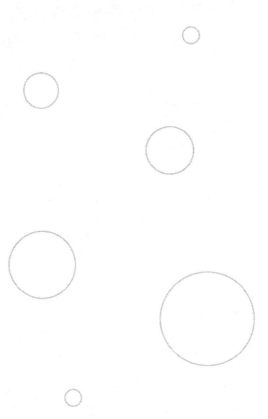

Notes